AN INVITATION TO

CHESS

A Picture Guide to
THE ROYAL GAME

By

Irving Chernev *and* Kenneth Harkness

A FIRESIDE BOOK
Published by Simon & Schuster, Inc.
NEW YORK

This Fireside Edition, 1985

Published by Simon & Schuster, Inc.
Simon & Schuster Building
Rockefeller Center
1230 Avenue of the Americas
New York, New York 10020

FIRESIDE and colophon are registered trademarks of
Simon & Schuster, Inc.

Manufactured in the United States of America

10 9 8 7 6 5 4 3   Pbk.

Library of Congress Cataloging in Publication Data

Chernev, Irving, date
    An invitation to chess.

    "A Fireside book."
    1. Chess. I. Harkness, Kenneth. II. Title.
GV1446.C47 1985   794.1'2   85-1721
ISBN: 0-671-21270-2 Pbk.

CONTENTS

FOREWORD

THIS little book is an invitation to the royal game of chess.

There is a widely held popular belief that chess is "too deep" for the average person. The idea that one has to be "brainy" to play the game is pure nonsense. No more brains are required to play this fascinating game than are needed to master contract bridge or gin rummy. There are millions of chess players in the world and most of them are just ordinary people of average intelligence. In Russia—where chess is as popular as baseball in the United States—children play chess almost before they learn to speak. In this country, chess is growing rapidly in popularity and is played by men and women of all ages. Thousands of children are playing the game in their homes and in school clubs.

It is true that the chess expert—or master, as he is called—can perform remarkable mental feats on the chessboard, but the same thing could be said of other games and sports. The contract bridge master, for instance, is able to make intricate plays which are far beyond the capacity of the average person—but this does not deter a great host of bridge players from enjoying their favorite indoor sport. Similarly, most chess players are incapable of executing the deep combinations and strategic maneuvers of the chessmaster, but they play their own brand of chess and enjoy it. The ordinary player is able to admire the beauty and art of master play, the amazing tactics and perfect timing displayed by these experts, but he plays with opponents of his own strength and enjoys his own games best of all.

We invite you to learn chess because it is by far the best two-handed game in existence. It is an exciting, thrilling game—a lifelong source of interest and amusement. An absorbing hobby, chess will provide you with relaxation and recreation in greater measure than any other home game.

And chess is not a slow game. Most friendly contests last about an hour—and every minute is packed full of interest for both players. If you like, you can play Lightning Chess, in which each player is allowed only ten seconds to make his move and the entire game is over in a few minutes.

Chess is easy to learn. The rules are explained in Part One of this book and are presented in a new way, originated by the authors. Photographs, diagrams and examples clarify each definition. With the aid of this visual method of instruction, you can learn how the chessmen move in a few minutes and master all the rules in one or two evenings. At the same time, the illustrations and examples will give you a working knowledge of the game so that you will be able to start playing just as soon as you have completed the first section of the book. Naturally, you will not be able to defeat somebody who has been playing chess for years, but you will be able to play with other beginners and thoroughly enjoy your battles, even though an expert might shudder at some of your moves. As you gain experience you will become more skillful and will be able to appreciate the finer points of the game.

When you finish Part One you will also understand "chess notation"—the simple code used by chess players to record the moves of games. In the past, this notation has been a stumbling block to those who have attempted to learn chess from books. At first sight, these mysterious symbols are incomprehensible. However, they are just abbreviations based on a simple method of naming the chessmen and the squares of the chessboard. The gradual and painless way in which chess notation is introduced and illustrated in this book will enable you to master it without conscious effort on your part.

A knowledge of chess notation is by no means essential. There are thousands of chess players who have never even heard of it. However, when you are able to read notation the entire field of chess literature is opened up. You can play over and enjoy games from master tournaments, as published in newspapers, chess magazines and books. Moreover, a knowledge of notation increases your skill. It gives you a familiarity with the squares of the board and helps you to think in the proper terms.

The second and third sections of this book are devoted to a thorough explanation of the basic principles of chess. Particular emphasis is laid on the fundamentals of the opening phase of the game, where beginners are most likely to go astray. Each principle is illustrated by examples. Entire games are reproduced and explained in detail. Unlike other chess books, you do not need to refer to a chessboard to understand these examples and illustrative games. You can follow them mentally with the aid of the diagrams showing the positions after each move or short series of moves. In fact, this is the first chess primer ever published which you can read in bed, in the subway, at home, or wherever you happen to be, without requiring a set of chessmen and chessboard to follow the text.

The phases of the game treated in this book are covered in great detail, in the belief that a thorough understanding of the basic principles is more beneficial than a superficial knowledge of all aspects of the game. A complete explanation of the strategy and tactics of the middle game and end game are beyond the scope of this work. The material in this book, however, will give you all the knowledge you need to play the game intelligently—and that is all we hope to accomplish in this invitation to chess.

IRVING CHERNEV
KENNETH HARKNESS

PART ONE

The Rules of Chess

THE CHESSMEN AND CHESSBOARD

To PLAY CHESS you need a set of chessmen and a chessboard. You may, if you wish, use an inexpensive pocket chess set; but eventually you will want to own a regular set of plastic or wooden chessmen and a cloth or wooden board.

Chessmen and boards are available in various sizes, colors and designs. If possible, take the advice of an experienced chessplayer in selecting your set. Tricky designs and violent colors become distasteful later. Although red and black boards are sold in great quantities, you will find more subdued colors easier on the eyes.

The pieces of a "Staunton design" plastic chess set are pictured on this page. On other pages, a wooden chess set of similar design is illustrated. With slight modifications in the products of different manufacturers, sets of this design are by far the most popular.

Let us now examine the chessmen in detail and take stock of the "White" and "Black" forces. No matter what the actual color of your chessmen may be, it is customary to refer to the light-colored men as the *white* pieces and the dark-colored men as the *black* pieces.

Comparing your chessmen with the illustration below, you will note that the white pieces consist of 1 King, 1 Queen, 2 Bishops, 2 Knights, 2 Rooks and 8 Pawns. Now if you compare the white with the black men you will find that they correspond exactly. There are two identical sets of forces—a White army and a Black army.

King   **Queen**   **Bishop**   **Knight**   **Rook**   **Pawn**

The two chess armies are lined up at the top of page 6 for your inspection. In this illustration the chessmen are represented by their *symbols*, as used in the diagrams throughout this book.

White Men			Black Men	
♚	1 King		♚	1 King
♛	1 Queen		♛	1 Queen
♝ ♝	2 Bishops		♝ ♝	2 Bishops
♞ ♞	2 Knights		♞ ♞	2 Knights
♜ ♜	2 Rooks		♜ ♜	2 Rooks
♟ ♟ ♟ ♟ ♟ ♟ ♟ ♟	8 Pawns		♟ ♟ ♟ ♟ ♟ ♟ ♟ ♟	8 Pawns

The Chessboard

Chess is played between two opponents on a board with 64 squares. Every square may be used. The board has 32 light and 32 dark squares. These are always referred to as *white* and *black* squares.

The board must be placed so that each player has a *white* square at the right hand corner nearest to him. (See pointer above.) This is important. You cannot play chess with the board turned round the wrong way.

THE STARTING LINE-UP

You ARE NOT yet ready to play a game of chess—but this picture shows how the chessmen must be lined up to start a game. Place the pieces on the board as explained under the diagrams below. Remember to place the board with a *white* square at the *right* hand corner nearest to you.

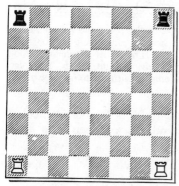

1 *Each player has two Rooks. Place them in the corners.*

2 *Each player has two Knights. They go next to the Rooks.*

3 Each player has two Bishops. Place them beside the Knights.

4 The White Queen goes on the remaining white square on the front row; the Black Queen goes on the corresponding black square on the back row.

5 Place the Kings beside the Queens. The opposing Kings and Queens directly face each other across the board. King opposite King; Queen opposite Queen.

6 Finally, place the pawns on the second rank, each in front of a piece. The board and men are now properly set up, ready for play. Compare with photo on page 7.

REMEMBER THIS RULE: The Queen always goes "on her own color" —*White* Queen on a *white* square and *Black* Queen on a *black* square.

The MOVES of the CHESSMEN

As THE PAINTER mixes his pigments and spreads them on canvas to create a work of art, so does the chess-master combine the distinctive powers of the chessmen to produce a masterpiece of the chessboard.

The art of chess is based on the fact that each *type* of man —King, Queen, Bishop, Knight, Rook and Pawn—moves in a different way, in accordance with definite rules. Each type has special powers, prescribed limitations.

At first sight, it may seem as though the chessmen swoop at each other from one side of the board to the other without rhyme or reason. Queens, Bishops and Rooks dart hither and yon. Knights leap from square to square in peculiar fashion. Actually, these pieces are following a clear-cut pattern, are moving and capturing in accordance with simple rules, pictured and described on the following pages. This pictorial presentation of the chess moves will enable you to comprehend the powers of the pieces *in a few minutes!*

The King moves **one square** at a time in **any direction.**

SEE PICTURE ABOVE. Here the King has 8 *optional moves.* He can move in any desired direction (indicated by the arrows) to any one of the 8 adjoining squares.

1 The King may capture an enemy piece on any square to which he has the option of moving. Here the White King can capture the Black Knight or the Black Pawn.

2 The King has captured the Knight. Note the method of capturing. The Knight is removed and the King occupies the square on which the Knight stood.

HOW THE ROOK MOVES AND CAPTURES

The Rook moves North, South, East or West. It may travel **any desired number of squares** in one move, provided there is no obstructing piece.

THE ROOK in the picture can move in the *directions* indicated by the arrows and it can *stop* at any of the squares marked with a white dot. If an enemy piece (Black, in this case) occupied one of the dotted squares, the Rook could *capture* it. If a friendly piece (White) occupied any of these squares, the Rook would be obstructed and could not move beyond the obstruction.

The *White* Rook in the diagram below can move to the *left* and capture the Bishop; or to the *right* and capture the Pawn; or it can move *up* and capture the Knight, or *down* and capture the Black Rook.

Chess captures are accomplished by removing the enemy piece and occupying the square on which it was standing.

The Bishop moves **diagonally**. It may travel **any desired number of squares** in one move, provided there is no obstruction.

THE BISHOP in the picture can move in the *directions* indicated by the arrows and it can stop at any of the dotted squares. Like the Rook, it can capture an enemy piece and would be obstructed by a friendly piece on any of these dotted squares.

The Bishop in the diagram below can move *up to the right* and capture the Rook or *up to the left* and capture the Queen; or it can move *down to the left* and capture the Knight or *down to the right* and capture the pawn.

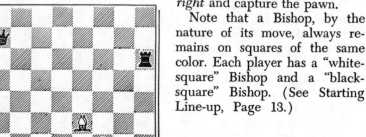

Note that a Bishop, by the nature of its move, always remains on squares of the same color. Each player has a "white-square" Bishop and a "black-square" Bishop. (See Starting Line-up, Page 13.)

HOW THE QUEEN MOVES AND CAPTURES

The Queen combines in one piece the moves of a **Rook** and **Bishop**.

THE QUEEN in the above photo can move in the *directions* indicated by the arrows and can *stop* at any of the squares marked with a white dot. The Queen could capture an enemy piece and would be obstructed by any friendly piece which occupied any of the dotted squares.

The Queen in this diagram can move like a Rook and capture either of the black pieces. The white men prevent her from moving in any other direction.

The Queen in this diagram can move like a Bishop and capture either of the black pieces. The white men prevent her from moving in any other direction.

19

The Knight **jumps over** friendly or enemy pieces. It **leaps one square** (to the North, South, East or West) and lands to the right or to the left **on a square of the opposite color** to the one from which it started.

THE KNIGHT leaps from a black square to a white square—or from a white square to a black square. *It always goes to a square of the opposite color.*

The Knight in the picture at the top of the page is on a black square. It can leap to any one of the eight white squares indicated by the dotted arrow tips and could capture an enemy unit located on any of these squares

The Knight in the picture at the left is on a white square. One of its eight possible moves is indicated by the arrow. This Knight can move only to black squares.

In common with all the other chessmen, the Knight cannot move to a square already occupied by one of its own men. Unlike the others, however, the Knight is never obstructed by pieces on intervening squares. When capturing, or when moving to a vacant square, *it leaps over any of its own men or any of its opponent's men.*

1 The White Knight can capture any of the 8 black pieces as they are all on squares to which the Knight has the option of moving.

2 This White Knight can also capture any of the 8 black pieces. Note that it now goes from a white to a black square.

3 The White Knight can jump over the Black Pawns and capture the Black Rook. Suppose they were its own pawns?

4 The Knight can still jump over them and capture the Black Rook. The Knight can jump over any pieces on intervening squares.

HOW THE PAWN MOVES

The Pawn is the soldier of chess. It marches straight forward—
one square at a time.

THE PAWN in the picture above has only *one move*. It can go
forward one square, as indicated by the arrow. It cannot move
backwards, nor in any other direction.

If a friendly piece were located on the square immediately in
front of this Pawn (the square indicated by the dotted arrow
tip), the Pawn would be *completely blocked* and could not
move. Moreover, the Pawn would be similarly obstructed by an
enemy piece on this square, because the Pawn, unlike other
pieces, does *not* capture as it moves. (The Pawn's method of capturing is described on page 24.)

The Pawn's Initial Move

On its **first move**, the Pawn has the **choice** of moving forward **one or two squares**. After the first move it may continue up the board, but only one square at a time.

THE EIGHT PAWNS in the picture above are lined up in their original positions at the beginning of the game. (See Starting Line-up.) From this starting position, each Pawn may move forward *either one or two squares*, as indicated by the dotted arrows.

Remember, it is only when the Pawn moves *for the first time* that it is permitted to go forward two squares. Furthermore, both squares must be vacant.

HOW THE PAWN CAPTURES

The Pawn can **capture** an enemy unit on either of the two squares
diagonally in front of the Pawn.

THE PAWN in the picture above can *capture* on either of the two
squares indicated by the arrows. The Pawn *cannot move to these
squares in the ordinary way;* but if an enemy unit were located
on either of the squares indicated by the dotted arrow tips, the
Pawn could *capture* it and thus reach one of these squares.

Observe that the Pawn's *move* and the Pawn's *capture* are entirely different. In this respect the Pawn is exceptional; all the
other chessmen capture in exactly the same way as they move.

Note particularly that the Pawn does *not* capture an enemy
unit in the path of its ordinary forward movement. Consequently,
a Pawn is *blocked* by any piece (friend or foe) standing on the
square directly in front of it.

The Pawn's method of capturing greatly increases its power.
Whereas it can move to only one square (after its first move) it
can capture on either one of *two* squares. Beginners are inclined
to forget this and often place their pieces on squares where they
can be captured by the opponent's Pawn. Bear in mind that the
Pawn captures "like a V."

Before Capturing

The Pawn can capture either the Rook or the Knight.

After Capturing

The Pawn has captured the Knight.

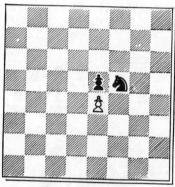

Before Capturing

Neither Pawn can capture the other Pawn—but the White Pawn can capture the Knight.

After Capturing

The White Pawn has captured the Knight and occupies the square on which the Knight stood.

How Pawns Move in Chess Diagrams

THE TWO MOVES pictured in the diagrams below are frequently used to start a game of chess. At the beginning of the game, the only pieces that can move are the Pawns and the Knights; all others are blocked.

In Diagram 1, *White* (the player handling the white pieces) has advanced his *King's Pawn* (the Pawn in front of his King) and thus unblocked his Queen and one of his Bishops (the King's Bishop—next to the King).

In Diagram 2, *Black* (the player handling the black pieces) has made the same move with his King's Pawn and similarly released his Queen and King's Bishop.

As each player moves his Pawns forward (towards his opponent) it follows that the white and black Pawns always move in opposite directions.

In chess diagrams, it is understood that the white Pawns move *up* the board and the black Pawns move *down* the board, unless stated to the contrary.

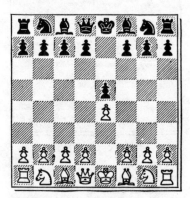

1 The White Pawn in the center has moved forward two squares. This is a popular and good opening move.

2 In reply, the Black Pawn has advanced two squares. Now these two Pawns block each other and neither can move.

OBSTRUCTIONS AND CAPTURES

WHEN A GAME of chess is in progress, the chessmen are at least partially obstructed by other pieces on the board. Except when making a capture, a piece can move only to a vacant square. When capturing, a piece occupies the square vacated by the captured piece.

When moving to a vacant square, or when making a capture, the Knight can leap over any intervening pieces, but the other chessmen cannot do this. The other men cannot move *beyond* an obstructing piece, friend or foe. This rule is illustrated in the following pictures and diagrams.

Unlike checkers, *captures are always optional.* If you attack an enemy piece and your opponent does not move it away, you are not obliged to capture on your next move, or later. If your opponent places a piece on a square where you can capture it, you may do so if you wish but it is not compulsory. The only exception to this rule is when a capture is the only move that can be made—the only legal move on the board. Then the player must make the capture, or resign the game.

The Knight can leap over the other men and capture the Queen, but the Knight is the only piece that can do this. Other types of men are obstructed by intervening pieces.

The Black Rook can capture the White Pawn or the White Bishop, but it cannot capture the Knight or Queen as it is not allowed to move beyond either of the Pawns.

The White Bishop can capture either of the Black Rooks, but it cannot capture the Knight as it is obstructed by a Pawn and is not allowed to move beyond this Pawn.

The White Queen can capture the Black Pawn or the Black Rook, but it cannot go beyond the Pawn and capture the Knight, nor go beyond the King and capture the Bishop.

The White Rook in this diagram is completely obstructed by its own men and cannot move at all. The Black Knight can leap over the white men and capture the Rook.

Here the Black Queen is completely hemmed in by the other men and cannot move. The White Knight can leap over and capture the Queen.

The White Queen Captures a Black Pawn

**Before
Capturing**

THE WHITE QUEEN is *obstructed* by her own pieces and can move only in *two directions*, as indicated by the arrows. She can move to any of the dotted squares, or she can capture the Black Pawn (but she cannot go beyond the Black Pawn).

**After
Capturing**

THE QUEEN has moved forward and *captured* the Black Pawn. The Pawn has been removed from the board and the Queen occupies the square on which the Pawn stood. The Queen was *not forced* to capture the Pawn. Chess captures are *optional*.

WHEN you have learned how the different types of chessmen move and capture, and how games are won or drawn, you possess the basic knowledge required to start playing chess. From the interesting and varying character of the moves, as described and pictured on the foregoing pages, you probably realize that chess is an extremely colorful, animated game. The uninitiated may look at the chessboard, while a game is in progress, and merely see inanimate pieces of wood on checkered squares; but to those who know the movements of the chessmen, the board is alive with potentialities. The all-powerful Queen radiates its strength in all directions; the Rooks and Bishops threaten enemy pieces on distant squares; the Knights keep their eyes on nearby posts, ready to leap over barricades and attack the enemy; the Pawns face each other across the board, each armed with a V-shaped prong with which to attack or defend.

HOW DO YOU WIN?

But what happens on the miniature battlefield of the chessboard? How is a decision reached?

The manner in which a game of chess is won is perhaps

the most interesting and distinctive feature of the entire game. The ultimate objective is the "checkmate" of the opponent's King. The King is checkmated (or "mated") when it is *subject to capture and there is no way of preventing this.* You have won the game if you are threatening to "take" your opponent's King and it is impossible for him to avert the capture. The King is never *actually* captured. You cannot take the King and go on playing; there is nothing left to play for. The game is over when the capture of one of the Kings cannot be prevented.

With the checkmate of the King as the determining factor, the end of a game of chess is unpredictable except in the last stages. Sometimes a direct attack on the King is made comparatively early in the proceedings and if the attack is successful the game is over in a few moves. At other times, no attempt is made to directly assault the King until most of the pieces have disappeared from the board by captures and recaptures (exchanges). Each game has distinctive and individual characteristics; except in rare instances, no two games are ever alike. Certain "openings" may be followed for a few moves (the players make a series of opening moves which have been recommended by chessmasters) but before long they are "on their own" and have to do their own thinking, their own planning.

HOW LONG DOES IT TAKE?

Contrary to general belief, the average game of chess does not last long. Most friendly games are over in less than an hour. Even tournament and match games between masters, with prizes or titles at stake, are usually finished in less than 4 hours, frequently in less than 3 hours. In many chess clubs, one of the most popular diversions is the "rapid transit" or "lightning chess" tournament, in which the players are allowed ten seconds for each move and a game lasts only a few minutes!

HOW THE GAME IS PLAYED

At this stage, we can describe the procedure only in general terms. The player with the white pieces *always starts first*; he makes the opening move. Then Black makes a move and the game continues with the players moving alternately. At no time may either player move twice in succession, or pass his move. Captures are not compulsory, nor are you required to inform your opponent that you threaten to capture one of his pieces at your next turn.

At the beginning of the game, the main object is to free the pieces for action, get them on to squares where they will exercise their power to the fullest advantage. The forces must be mobilized for the ensuing battle. As the game proceeds, various strategical plans are made which the players try to carry out. The forces are combined to launch an attack or to defend against the onslaughts of the enemy. At all times, the players bear in mind the final and all-important objective—the checkmating of the King. Each safeguards his own King, attempts to weaken the defenses of the opponent's King. Sometimes an all-out attack is made in an attempt to force an early checkmate. More frequently, the player concentrates his attack on some weak point in the opponent's position and eventually may succeed in reducing the strength of the enemy by winning a Pawn or a more important piece. This gives him a definite advantage, often sufficient to win the game. Throughout the proceedings, pieces are constantly being exchanged and the player must carefully "guard" each of his units so that he will not "lose a piece" if a capture is made by the opponent.

In some games, the players exchange their pieces without advantage to either side and the forces dwindle to the point at which neither player can force checkmate. Such games are drawn as no decision can be reached. There are other conditions under which games are drawn, to be explained later.

CHECK AND CHECKMATE

Before we describe and illustrate an actual game of chess, it is necessary for the learner to clearly understand what it means to "check" the King, how the King can get "out of check" and the specific meaning of "checkmate." A pictorial explanation of these terms is given on the following pages.

CHECKING THE KING

WHEN THE King is attacked and subject to capture, he is said to be "in check." The player who attacks the King calls out "check" as a warning and *all other business must be dropped.* The King must immediately be removed from check. No matter what else may be taking place on the board, the King's plight takes priority. Any move which does not remove the King from check is an *illegal move* and must be retracted.

Any piece may check the King except the opposing King. The diagrams on these pages show examples of checks by the Queen, Rook, Bishop, Knight and Pawn, together with an illustration of "discovered check" and "double check."

An ordinary check is made by moving a piece to a square from which it attacks the King. A "discovered check" is accomplished by making a move which unmasks an attack on the King by *another* piece. A "double check" is a simultaneous attack on the King by two pieces. The player checks the King with one piece and releases a discovered check by another piece.

1 The King is in the line of capture of the Queen. He is therefore in check. In this case the Queen is attacking diagonally, like a Bishop.

2 The Rook moves North, South, East or West. It is therefore attacking, or checking the King. Here the direction of the Rook's attack is due north.

3 Here the King is subject to capture by the Bishop. The Bishop moves and captures diagonally. The King is in check.

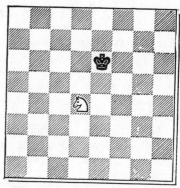

4 The Knight is attacking or checking the King. The Knight leaps over to a square of the opposite color.

5 The King is in check as the Pawn attacks and captures diagonally, one square ahead.

6 Here the King is NOT in check but if the Bishop moves it will unmask a "discovered check" by the Rook.

IF THE Bishop in diagram 6 moves 3 squares up, in a diagonal direction, *both the Bishop and Rook will be checking the King.* When the King is attacked simultaneously by two pieces in this manner, it is said to be in "double check."

GETTING OUT OF CHECK

THE PLAYER whose King is in check must make a move which will remove his King from check. *Any other move would be illegal.*

There are three ways of getting out of check:

1. *Moving the King to a square on which he is no longer in check.* This method is illustrated in diagrams 1A and 1B.

Note that it is not sufficient to move the King to another square on which he would *still* be in check. He must move to a square on which he is not attacked by the checking piece *or by any other piece.*

When the King is in "double check" (checked by two pieces) he *must* move. The remaining two methods would not enable him to get out of check.

2. *Capturing the checking piece.* This method is illustrated in diagrams 2A and 2B. The King stays where he is and the check is removed by capturing the checking piece.

3. *Placing a piece between the King and the checking piece.* This method is illustrated in diagrams 3A and 3B. Again the King stays where he is and the check is removed by interposing a piece to ward off the attack.

Note that this method does not avail against check by a Knight as the Knight leaps over intervening pieces. When a Knight checks the King, the Knight must be captured or the King must be moved out of check.

King Is in Check

1A The Rook is checking the King. The direction of the Rook's attack is due North.

King Is Out of Check

1B To get out of check, the King simply steps away from the line of attack.

King Is in Check

2A He can get out of check by stepping away (as in 1B) or the Bishop can capture the checking Rook.

King Is Out of Check

2B The Rook has been captured and as it has been removed from the board the King is no longer in check.

King Is in Check

3A He can get out of check by moving away (as in 1B) or the Black Rook can be interposed to break up the attack.

King Is Out of Check

3B The King is not in check as his own Rook is a barrier between himself and the White Rook.

IT FREQUENTLY happens that the player whose King is in check can choose between the three methods described above. Two or three of these ways of getting out of check may be available. In such cases, the player may select whichever method he prefers. Of course, if only one method is possible, he must get out of check by the only available means.

CHECKMATING THE KING

If the King is in check and it is impossible to get him out of check by any of the three methods described on the previous pages, the King is checkmated and the player thus checkmated *has lost the game*. A player may have twice as many pieces as his opponent, but *if his King cannot get out of check he is checkmated and has lost the game.*

A typical checkmate is pictured in the photo above. Here the White King is "mated" (the shorter term is commonly used). The conditions of checkmate are fulfilled as follows:

The King is in check:

The Black Queen is attacking the King (diagonally) and is threatening to capture it.

The King cannot MOVE out of check:

The only square to which the King can move is the corner square and here the King would *still* be in check by the Queen. The move would be illegal.

The checking piece cannot be captured:

The only piece capable of capturing the Queen is the King itself: but if the King captured the Queen it would then be in check from the Black Bishop. Hence, the capture would *not* get the King out of check. The capture would be illegal. (No move or capture can ever be made which exposes the King to a check.)

Nothing can be interposed between the checking piece and the King.

Other examples of checkmates are given below.

1 The Black King is checkmated. He is attacked by the Queen and no matter where he moves, he would still be attacked by the Rook or Queen.

2 Here the King cannot move anywhere as he would still be in check from the Rook or Bishop. He cannot capture the Rook as he would then be in check from the Bishop. He is checkmated.

3 Checkmate. The Rook is checking the King and the latter cannot move out of the Rook's path. The Queen cannot be interposed between the King and Rook as the King would then be in check from the Bishop.

4 A checkmate by the Knight. The Knight is checking the King and the King cannot move. Black is not allowed to capture the Knight with his Pawn as the King would then be exposed to check by the Queen.

5 A checkmate by two Bishops. The Bishop on the black square is checking the King. The other Bishop and the White King are preventing the Black King from moving out of check.

6 Checkmate by a Knight. This type of mate is called a "smothered" mate. Only one piece is used to deliver checkmate. The King is smothered by his own men and cannot get out of check.

7 Checkmate by a Queen and Bishop. The White Queen is checking the King and cannot be captured because it is guarded by a Bishop. The Black King cannot move out of check, the only escape square being occupied by one of his own men.

8 Checkmate by a Rook guarded by a Knight. The Rook is checking the King and cannot be captured. The King is mated because he cannot move out of check. The white square is controlled by the Rook, the black square by the Knight.

$$\boxed{\begin{array}{c} \textit{MOVIE} \\[2mm] \textit{of a} \\[2mm] \textit{CHESS GAME} \end{array}}$$

W E STILL have a few more rules to learn, but first let us see what a real game of chess looks like.

On the following pages, we present a short "movie" of a chess game! Each and every move, from the opening to the final checkmate, is pictured in this series of photographs. Look for the arrow on each picture; it shows how the piece moves. You do not need a set of chessmen to follow this game as the pictures and comments tell the whole story. However, it will do no harm to play over the game on your chessboard or pocket set.

The game presented here was actually played many years ago in a chess tournament. In these events, the players always write down their moves on a "score-sheet." Written records of the games are thus preserved and important games are published in newspapers, magazines and books.

To enable players to write their moves quickly and to permit the publication of games in compact form, a simple "code" of symbols and abbreviations has been developed. Under the comment on each move in the following game, we briefly explain how chess-players would record the move in what is known as "descriptive chess notation."

HOW THE CHESSMEN ARE NAMED

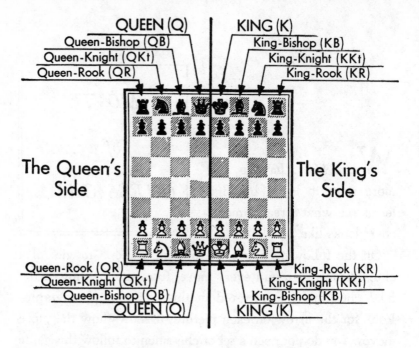

IN THE "movie" of a chess game which appears on the following pages, we refer to the pieces as the King-Rook, Queen-Bishop, King-Knight, etc. This means of identifying the men is explained in the above illustration.

In this diagram of the starting line-up, the chessboard is divided into two sections by the heavy line drawn down the middle of the board. The area to the left of this line is called the "Queen's side" of the board and the men in this area are known as Queen-side pieces. The area to the right is called the "King's side" and the men in this area are King-side pieces.

Each player has two Rooks, two Knights and two Bishops. These pieces, on the Queen's side, are called the Queen-Rook, Queen-Knight and Queen-Bishop. The corresponding pieces on the King's side are called the King-Rook, King-Knight and King-Bishop.

Each player has eight Pawns and these are identified by naming them after the "files" on which they stand. (Each vertical row of squares, up and down the board, is called a "file.") From left to right in the above diagram, the Pawns (White or Black) are called the Queen-Rook's Pawn, Queen-Knight's Pawn, Queen-

Bishop's Pawn, Queen's Pawn, King's Pawn, King-Bishop's Pawn, King-Knight's Pawn and King-Rook's Pawn.

If a Pawn captures and thereby moves to an adjoining file, it takes the name of the file to which it has moved. For instance, if a Queen-Rook's Pawn captures an enemy man on the Queen-Knight's file, it is then referred to as a Queen-Knight's Pawn.

When describing the moves of a chess game, it is customary to use initials instead of the full names of the pieces. Thus, K stands for King, Q for Queen, B for Bishop, Kt for Knight*, R for Rook and P for Pawn. The initials used for Queen-Rook (QR), Queen-Knight (QKt), etc. are shown in the diagram. In the same way, Queen-Rook's Pawn is represented by QRP, Queen-Knight's Pawn by QKtP, etc.

---

* In some chess literature, the Knight is represented by the symbol N, to avoid confusion between K for King and Kt for Knight. In this book, however, we adhere to the classical Kt for Knight.

White's First Move

White starts this game by moving his King's Pawn two squares forward. Note that his Queen and one of his Bishops can now get into action.

IN THE LANGUAGE of chess, this move is described as "Pawn to King 4"—meaning that the Pawn has moved to the 4th square in front of the King (counting the square on which the King stands as No. 1).

To write down the move, initials are used for Pawn (P) and King (K) so that it appears as follows:

Move No.   White   Black
    1   P–K4   . . .

The dash between P and K4 means "to" or "moves to."

The diagram at the left shows the same position as pictured above. Each move of this game is illustrated by a photograph and diagram.

Black's First Move

Black begins by bringing out his Queen-Knight which leaps over the Pawns and is ready for further action.

BLACK'S MOVE is called "Knight to Queen-Bishop 3." In other words, the Knight has moved to the 3rd square in front of Black's Queen-Bishop (counting the square on which the Bishop stands as No. 1).

Using abbreviations (Kt for Knight and QB3 for Queen-Bishop 3) the move is written:

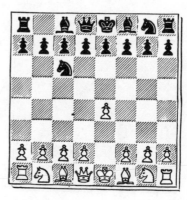

    White   Black
   1 . . .   *Kt–QB3*

The dots after the move number indicate that White's move has already been recorded.

White advances his Queen's Pawn two squares, giving his Queen still more scope and unblocking his other Bishop. Both Bishops are now free to move.

WHITE'S MOVE is "Pawn to Queen 4." The Pawn moves to the 4th square in front of the Queen. (The Queen's square is Queen 1.) Using initials, the move is written:

2 P–Q4 . . .

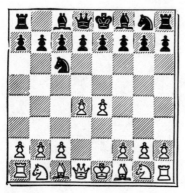

When recording a *White* move, the *number* of the square is obtained by starting the count from *White's* first rank (the bottom row in the pictures). When recording a *Black* move, the count starts from *Black's* first rank (the top of the board).

Each row of squares running across the board (East and West) is called a "Rank."

Black's Second Move

Black moves his King's Pawn two squares. Black is now attacking the White Queen's Pawn with both Knight and Pawn. White must decide what to do about this.

THIS MOVE is "Pawn to King 4" and is written:

> 2 . . .   *P–K4*

The Pawn moves to the 4th square in front of the King. A more accurate way of expressing this is to say that the Pawn moves to the 4th square on the *King's file*. The vertical rows of squares (up and down the board) are called "files" and are named after the pieces at the top and bottom of each file in the starting line-up. (The opposing Kings are at the top and bottom of the King's file; the two Queens are at the top and bottom of the Queen's file, etc.)

White's Third Move

White advances his Queen's Pawn one square forward. Now the White Pawn attacks and threatens to capture the Black Knight.

NOTE THAT White had various choices on this move—which is typical of chess. He could have captured Black's Pawn with his own Pawn—or permitted Black to capture. Instead he decided to move the threatened Pawn.

White's move is called "Pawn to Queen 5" and is written:

3 P–Q5 . .

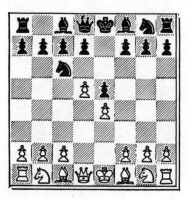

Square Q5 (Queen 5) is the fifth on the Queen's file, counting from White's first rank at the bottom of the board.

Black's Third Move

Black does not want to lose his Knight—so he moves it away.

A KNIGHT is much more valuable than a Pawn. If Black had not moved his Knight, White would have captured it; and although Black could then take the capturing Pawn, the exchange would be all in White's favor.

Black's move is "Queen-Knight to King 2." In abbreviated form, this is written:

   3 . . .   QKt–K2

As *either* of Black's Knights could have moved to square K2 (the 2nd square on the King's file) it is necessary to specify that the Queen-Knight (QKt) was moved.

White moves his King-Bishop's Pawn two squares forward. This Pawn now attacks the advanced Black Pawn.

EACH PAWN bears the name of the file on which it stands. The Pawn moved by White is called the King-Bishop's Pawn because it stands on the King-Bishop's file—the vertical row of squares between the White King-Bishop and the Black King-Bishop in the starting line-up.

The move is described as "Pawn to King-Bishop 4" or Pawn to the 4th square on the King-Bishop's file and is written:

4 P–KB4   ...

Black's Fourth Move

Black moves his Queen's Pawn one square. In this way he defends his King's Pawn, attacked by White. If White captures the King's Pawn, the Pawn just moved can capture in return.

BLACK'S 4TH move is "Pawn to Queen 3" or Pawn to the 3rd square on the Queen's file, counting from the top of the board (the Black side).

Here is the "score" of the game up to this point:

White	Black
1 P–K4	Kt–QB3
2 P–Q4	P–K4
3 P–Q5	QKt–K2
4 P–KB4	P–Q3

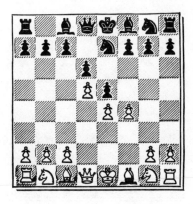

You have probably seen chess games recorded in this manner in newspapers and magazines. An entire game can be printed in a small space.

White brings his King-Knight into play. In its new position, the Knight attacks the Black King's Pawn, already threatened by the White King-Bishop's Pawn.

THE BLACK Pawn is attacked twice, defended once. White thus threatens to win a Pawn.

White's 5th move is called "Knight to King-Bishop 3" or Knight to the 3rd square on the King-Bishop's file and is written:

5 Kt–KB3   . . .

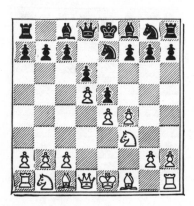

The names of the files are permanent. For instance, the King-Bishop's file is always called the King-Bishop's file, no matter where the Bishops may move later in the game.

Black's Fifth Move

Black moves his Bishop and "pins" the White Knight. If the Knight were to move, the Bishop could capture White's all-powerful Queen.

BLACK THUS defends his threatened King's Pawn indirectly by making it unprofitable for White to capture with his Knight. Black would gladly give up his Pawn and Bishop to gain the White Queen.

Black's move is written:

5 . . .   B–Kt5

Unnecessary details are always omitted. Black can move only one of his Bishops and there is only one Kt5 square to which this Bishop can move —the 5th square on the King-Knight's file. Hence, "Bishop to Knight 5" is sufficient. It is not necessary and not good practice to write this move as 5 . . . B–KKt5.

White "develops" his other Knight—which means that he brings it into play.

WHITE MAKES no specific or immediate threat with this move. He is mobilizing his forces.

The move is called "Knight to Bishop 3" and is written:

6 Kt–B3   . . .

Again observe the omission of unnecessary details. The 3rd square on the *King*-Bishop's file (KB3) is already occupied and

"B3" is therefore sufficient to identify the square on the Queen-Bishop file to which the Knight is moved. As only one Knight can move to this square, Kt–B3 is adequate. It is unnecessary and redundant to record this move as 6 Kt–QB3 or 6 QKt–B3.

Black's Sixth Move

Black moves his Knight and attacks the White King-Bishop's Pawn.

THE WHITE Pawn is now attacked twice as Black is also threatening to capture it with his King's Pawn.

Black's 6th move is called "Knight to Knight 3" and is written:

6 . . .   Kt–Kt3

Actually, it is the *Queen*-Knight which moves to the 3rd square on the *King*-Knight's file—but it is not necessary to give these specifications. The simple "Kt–Kt3" identifies the move without any possibility of confusion. This move should not be written as 6 . . . Kt–KKt3 or 6 . . . QKt–Kt3.

White counter-attacks and threatens to capture the Black Bishop
by moving his King-Rook's Pawn one square forward.

As IN war, the counter-attack is frequently used in chess. Instead
of guarding his threatened Pawn, White makes a counter-threat
which cannot be ignored without loss, a Bishop being more valuable than a Pawn.

White's 7th move is "Pawn to King-Rook 3." This is written:

7 P–KR3   . . .

Here the square must be
clearly identified as *King*-
Rook 3 (KR3). To write "P–
R3" would be ambiguous as
White could play P–QR3 or
P–KR3. Note that the prefix K
or Q is only used in cases like
this, when it is *necessary* to
indicate whether a King-side
or Queen-side square is intended.

Black's Seventh Move

Black captures the Knight with his Bishop.

THE WHITE Knight is removed from the board and the Black Bishop occupies the square on which the Knight stood. Black now threatens to capture the White Queen on his next move.

Black's 7th move is described as "Bishop takes Knight" and is recorded as follows:

7 . . .   BxKt

The symbol "x" stands for "takes" or "captures."

The score of the game, up to this move, in chess notation:

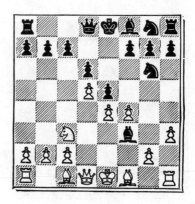

White	Black
1 P–K4	Kt–QB3
2 P–Q4	P–K4
3 P–Q5	QKt–K2
4 P–KB4	P–Q3
5 Kt–KB3	B–Kt5
6 Kt–B3	Kt–Kt3
7 P–KR3	BxKt

White's Eighth Move

White moves his Bishop to a square on which it attacks the King. The White player calls out "check!" Black must drop everything and get his King out of check.

A CHECK is the most effective of all counter-attacks—one which *must* be answered. White can leave his Queen "on take" because he knows that Black is not allowed to capture it while his King is in check.

White's move is known as "Bishop to Knight 5 check." The Bishop goes to the 5th square on the Queen-Knight's file and checks the King. The move is written:

8 B–Kt5ch   . . .

The word check is abbreviated to "ch."

Black's Eighth Move

Black advances his Queen-Bishop's Pawn one square, interposing it between his King and the checking Bishop. His King is now out of check.

BLACK COULD not capture the checking Bishop but he could have moved his King to get out of check. However, he preferred the third method and interposed one of his Pawns.

Black's move is called "Pawn to Bishop 3" and is written:

8 . . .   P–B3

The Pawn is moved to the 3rd square on the *Queen-Bishop's* file. However, "Pawn to Bishop 3" clearly identifies the move because this could not mean "Pawn to *King-Bishop 3*"—an illegal move. Hence, 8 . . . P–B3 is sufficient. It is not necessary to write 8 . . . P–QB3.

White captures the Black Pawn with his Queen's Pawn! Has White forgotten that his Queen is attacked by the Black Bishop?

WHITE'S MOVE can be described as "Pawn takes Bishop's Pawn" or "Queen's Pawn takes Pawn." Using the latter, the move is written:

9 QPxP . . .

Equally correct is 9 PxBP. However, the capture must be

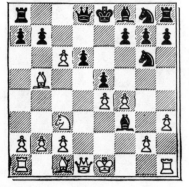

clearly identified. "Pawn takes Pawn" (9 PxP) would be insufficient as White has two possible Pawn captures on the board (the King-Bishop's Pawn can also capture a Pawn). In cases like this, it is necessary to identify the capture by naming the capturing Pawn or the captured Pawn.

Black captures the powerful Queen with his Bishop. The Queen is removed from the board and the Bishop takes its place.

THIS IS an example of the interesting "combinations" which take place in a chess game. Actually, White has not overlooked this capture. He has planned ahead and knows that if Black takes the Queen, White will *win the game.*

Black's 9th move (a capture is also called a "move") is described as "Bishop takes Queen" and is written:

9 . . .   *BxQ*

Can you see what the next move will be?

White's Pawn captures the Black Queen-Knight's Pawn and as the Bishop now attacks the King, White calls out "check!"

THIS IS another example of a "discovered" check. The attack on the King by the Bishop was unmasked by capturing with the White Pawn which stood between the Bishop and the King.

White's 10th move is called "Pawn takes Pawn check" and is written:

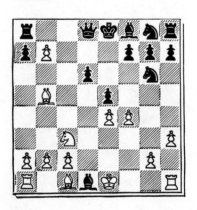

10 PxPch   . . .

This is sometimes written "10 PxPdis.ch." to show that it was a discovered check—but this is not essential. Nor is it necessary to write "Px KtPch" as no other Pawn capture delivers check.

Black's Tenth Move

Black gets his King out of check by moving him away from the Bishop's diagonal attack.

BLACK COULD have interposed his Queen between the Bishop and King and this would have prolonged the game by a few moves but Black's doom is sealed.

Black moved his King to the square K2 (King 2). The move is written:

10 . . .   K–K2

Here is the complete score of the game up to this point:

	White	Black
1	P–K4	Kt–QB3
2	P–Q4	P–K4
3	P–Q5	QKt–K2
4	P–KB4	P–Q3
5	Kt–KB3	B–Kt5
6	Kt–B3	Kt–Kt3
7	P–KR3	BxKt
8	B–Kt5ch	P–B3
9	QPxP	BxQ
10	PxPch	K–K2

Now White has a strong move. Can you foresee it?

White's Eleventh Move

White moves his Knight, checking the King.

WHITE IS closing in for the kill. His Knight leaps to the attack and forces the enemy King to come forward and meet his doom. Having "sacrificed" his Queen, the most valuable of all his pieces, White must make forceful moves and give his opponent's King no opportunity to escape.

Black now realizes that his capture of the White Queen was a mistake. This capture made it possible for White to launch an attack on the Black King.

White's move is "Knight to Queen 5 check." The Knight leaps to the 5th square on the Queen's file and attacks the King. The move is written:

11 Kt–Q5ch   ...

Now Black has only one legal move. What is the move?

Black's Eleventh Move

Black moves his King one square forward, to get out of check.

THIS MOVE was "forced." When a Knight checks, the Knight must be captured or the King must move. Here Black could not capture the Knight and the King was forced to move to the only square on which he is no longer in check.

Black's 11th move is "King to King 3" and is written:

11 . . .   K–K3

Before turning the page, examine this position carefully and see if you can select White's next move. Note that Black's King is hemmed in by White's forces. The King cannot move to a vacant square as he would be moving into check. For the same reason, he cannot capture the Knight. White can now deliver the final thrust.

White moves his King-Bishop's Pawn one square forward and announces "checkmate!" The game is over and White wins.

THE WHITE Pawn is checking the King and the King *cannot get out of check*. He cannot move to an unoccupied square as he would *still* be in check from the Bishop or Knight. Nor can he capture the checking Pawn or the White Knight as both are guarded by the White King's Pawn. Either capture would be

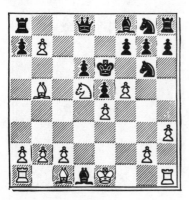

illegal. The checking Pawn cannot be captured by any other Black unit and interposition is impossible. Therefore, the King is checkmated.

White's final move is "Pawn to Bishop 5 mate" and is written:

12 P–B5 mate.

IN THE game just presented, Black was checkmated because he did not observe one of the fundamental principles of chess. *He failed to consider the safety of his King.* On the 7th move, Black should have retreated his Bishop to the square Q2, in front of his Queen. This would have protected his King from danger. By capturing the Knight, Black exposed his King to a dangerous attack which resulted in the loss of the game.

As the entire outcome of a game of chess depends on the fate of the King, the following rule should always be observed:

When it is your turn to move, avoid making any move which will give your opponent an opportunity to attack your King unless you are quite certain that the attack will be harmless.

As you gain knowledge and experience, you will be able to judge whether an attack on your King is harmless or not. In the meantime, regard with suspicion any contemplated move which will permit an attack on your King. Always consider the safety of your King and see that he is adequately protected.

The King is particularly vulnerable in the early stages of the game. On his original square he is in a comparatively exposed position and subject to attack. It is extremely important, therefore, that the player avoid making opening moves which will expose his King to danger. Furthermore, the King should be moved to a place of safety as quickly as possible.

A special move with King and Rook, known as "Castling," is described on the following pages. The main purpose of this move is to enable the player to quickly remove his King to a safe haven.

Other rules concerning the King are also covered in this section.

HOW TO CASTLE WITH KING AND ROOK

Castling with the **King-Rook.**

To ENABLE the player to quickly remove his King to a safe location, a maneuver known as "castling" is permitted under the rules of chess.

Castling involves the movement of two pieces (King and Rook) but *counts as one move.* Each player is allowed to make this combined move only *once* during the game.

There are two methods of castling, as illustrated by the two photos on these pages. The player has the choice of castling by either of these methods.

In each case, the King moves *two squares* (to the right, or to the left) and the Rook towards which he moves is transferred to the adjacent square on the other side of the King.

The picture at the top of this page illustrates the method known as "Castling on the King's side" or "Castling King's Rook." Here White moves his King *two squares* towards the **King-Rook** and transfers this Rook to the adjacent square on the other side of the King.

The picture on the next page illustrates "Castling on the Queen's side" or "Castling Queen's Rook." The King is moved *two squares* towards the **Queen-Rook** and the latter is placed on the other side of the King.

When recording a game by means of chess notation, special symbols are used for the castling moves. If a player "castles KR (King-Rook)" the move is represented by the symbol O–O. If he "castles QR (Queen-Rook)" the symbol O–O–O is used.

Castling with the **Queen-Rook.**

1 In this position, neither player has castled. (For the sake of clarity, other pieces normally on the board prior to castling are not shown.)

2 Now White has castled on the King's side. And Black has castled on the Queen's side. King-side castling is safer as a rule.

RULES ON CASTLING

CASTLING is an important safety privilege allowed to each player *only once* during a game. However, the player must observe the rules governing this move. There are certain conditions under which castling is not permitted; and others under which the right to castle is entirely forfeited.

The rules on castling are as follows:

(a) The squares between the King and Rook used for castling must be unoccupied. Otherwise, castling is illegal. See diagram 1.

(b) As any move which exposes the King to a check is illegal, castling is not permitted if it would cause the King to occupy, *or pass over*, a square attacked by an enemy man. See diagrams 2 and 3.

(c) If the King is in check, he is not permitted to castle out of check. See diagram 4. (This rule is frequently misinterpreted. The fact that the King *has* been checked does *not* deny him the right to castle later in the game. Moreover, the rules *permit* castling with a Rook attacked by an enemy man.)

(d) If the King has moved from his original square, the right to castle is entirely forfeited. See diagram 5. (Even if the King moves *back* to his original square, castling is no longer permitted.)

(e) If one of the Rooks has moved, the right to castle *with that Rook* is entirely forfeited. See diagram 6.

1 To castle, the squares between the King and Rook must be unoccupied. In above position, White cannot castle on either side; Black can castle on the King's side, but not on the Queen's side.

2 Castling into check is illegal. Here White is not permitted to castle as this would cause the King to occupy a square attacked by the Black Bishop.

71

3 Castling over check is illegal. Here White is not permitted to castle as the King would have to pass over a square controlled by the enemy Bishop.

4 Castling out of check is illegal. Here the White King is in check and is not permitted to castle to get out of check. He must get out of check by legal methods.

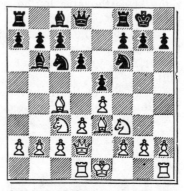

5 The White King has moved from his original square and has thereby forfeited the right to castle. The castling privilege is lost entirely, once the King has moved. Note that Black is getting ready to castle.

6 If a Rook has moved, the right to castle with that Rook is forfeited. In this position, White may castle with the King-Rook, but not with the Queen-Rook which has moved from its square.

CASTLE EARLY IN THE GAME

MANY CHESS GAMES are lost as a direct result of delay in castling. A player who fails to castle *at the earliest opportunity* is taking unnecessary risks and may lose the game on this account. An uncastled King is exposed to attacks from all angles and his presence in the center of the board is a constant source of danger. The learner should make a practice of castling *as soon as possible.*

The preferred and safest method of castling is *on the King's side.* Surrounded by unmoved Pawns and other protecting men, the King is more secure against attack on the King's side of the board. The learner should emulate the example of experts who choose this method of castling in the vast majority of their games. It requires considerable experience to recognize the special situations in which Queen-side castling can be used to advantage.

The King should be castled quickly because it is vulnerable to attack in the center. Opening moves which expose the King to attack must be avoided. In these 3 diagrams we illustrate the "Fool's Mate"—a striking example of how not to play chess.

1 In the "Fool's Mate" White exposes his King to danger by playing 1 P–KB3. Black plays P–K3.

2 White completely disregards the safety of his King by continuing 2 P–KKt4.

3 Black ends the "game" with 2 ...Q–R5 mate! An extreme example of careless play in the opening.

73

Illustrative Game

ANOTHER SHORT GAME is depicted in the following move-by-move diagrams. This game illustrates the dangerous attacks to which the King may be exposed if it is not castled and if Pawns are moved which permit the opponent to assault the King with his Queen and Bishops.

This game will also give you an opportunity to check your understanding of descriptive chess notation. Under each diagram the move depicted is written in standard notation, without comment.

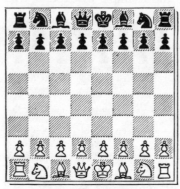

The starting position

White plays 1 P–K4

Black plays 1...P–QKt3

White plays 2 P–Q4

Black plays 2 ... B–Kt2

White plays 3 B–Q3

Black plays 3 ... P–KB4

White plays 4 P x P

Black plays 4 ... B x P

White plays 5 Q–R5ch

Black plays 5 ... P–Kt3

White plays 6 P x P

Black plays 6 ... Kt–KB3

White plays 7 P x P dis.ch

Black plays 7 ... Kt x Q

White plays 8 B–Kt6 mate

ILLEGAL EXPOSURE TO CHECK

THE LEARNER is again reminded that any move (including a capture) which exposes the King to a check is *illegal* and must be retracted. This rule is illustrated in the positions below.

1 The King is never permitted to move (or capture) into check and any move by another piece which exposes the King to check is an illegal move. In the above position, any move by the White Knight, Bishop or Pawn would be illegal. These pieces are said to be "pinned."

2 Here the White King is not permitted to move to either of the adjoining white squares. This would be moving into check in spite of the fact that the Black Bishop is completely pinned. A check is valid, even when made by a piece with no legal moves.

3 This is an illegal position. The two Kings are mutually attacking each other, which is impossible. A King cannot attack the opposing King; to do so, he would have to move into check. Consequently, the opposing Kings must always be separated by at least one square.

4 The White King is not allowed to castle on the Queen's side because this would cause the King to occupy a square adjoining the Black King—which is illegal. Kings can never occupy adjoining squares.

The POWER of the PAWN

YOU have undoubtedly seen many references to the "lowly Pawn" in literature and the daily press. Writers are fond of describing unwitting tools or those pre-destined to some dire fate as "mere Pawns."

It is true that the Pawn is the weakest of all the chessmen. While the Knights go leaping about the board and the Bishops, Rooks and Queens swing from one side to the other, the Pawn plods ahead one square at a time. His V-shaped capturing power adds to his strength and he is invaluable for defense, but the Pawn's scope is limited.

However, the Pawn is the one and only chessman with a real future ahead of him. He starts life at the lowest rung in the ladder of chess but he can look forward to promotion when he reaches his goal—which is something none of the other men can do.

On the following pages we explain the promotion power of the Pawn—and the rules governing a special type of Pawn capture.

PAWN PROMOTION

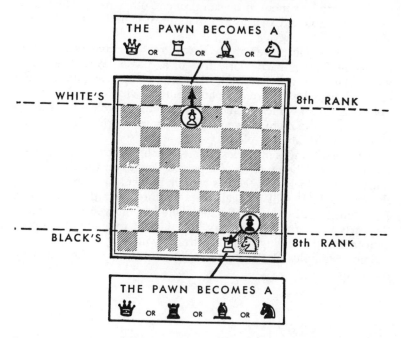

IF A PAWN succeeds in reaching the 8th rank, it immediately becomes a Queen, Rook, Knight or Bishop! The player who successfully advances a Pawn to his 8th rank immediately substitutes one of these pieces for the Pawn. The choice of pieces is up to the player but he *must* make the substitution. On reaching the 8th rank a Pawn cannot remain a Pawn. Another piece of the same color must be substituted—any piece but a King.

A Queen is usually selected as she is the most powerful piece and this promotion is called "Queening a Pawn." The term "under-promotion" is used if a player selects one of the less valuable pieces—a Rook, Knight or Bishop.

As illustrated in the diagram, a Pawn can reach the 8th rank by moving there in the ordinary way or by capturing an enemy unit. Thus, the White Pawn in the diagram can advance one square and on reaching the 8th rank it is immediately promoted to a White Queen, Rook, Bishop or Knight. The Black Pawn can reach the 8th rank by capturing the White Rook. Upon making this capture, the Pawn is immediately promoted to a Black Queen, Rook, Bishop or Knight.

Pawn promotion is not affected by the presence or absence of similar pieces on the board. For instance, if a player has his original Queen and promotes a Pawn he can have two Queens on the board—or more, if he can promote other pawns. Similarly, he can promote a Pawn to a Bishop, even if he has two Bishops already on the board.

The promotion power of the Pawn greatly enhances its potential value. This is particularly true of a "passed Pawn"—a Pawn which has passed beyond the barricade of opposing Pawns and can no longer be captured by an enemy Pawn. Such a Pawn is a potential threat which cannot be ignored. The closer it gets to the 8th rank the more dangerous it becomes. Its progress must be blocked with valuable pieces.

In the final stages of a chess game, much of the play frequently hinges around the creation of a passed Pawn and the subsequent removal of blockading pieces which prevent it from reaching the 8th rank. It will be realized, therefore, that the value of a Pawn must not be underestimated. The loss of even one Pawn in the early part of the game may be sufficient to enable the opponent to win the ending with his extra Pawn.

Some examples of Pawn promotion are given in the following diagrams.

1A *It is White's turn to move and he advances his Queen's Pawn one square to the eighth rank.*

1B *He substitutes a Queen for the promoted Pawn and thus checkmates the Black King.*

2A *It is White's move. He could not win by promoting his Pawn to a Queen. In fact, should he do so, the Black Queen would swoop down the file and checkmate him!*

2B *Instead, White under-promotes the Pawn to a Knight and checks the King which must move out of check. Note that after the King moves, White captures the Queen with his Knight.*

3A *If White's Pawn were to advance, the Bishop would simply capture it at once.*

3B *Instead, White captures the Knight, promoting the Pawn to a Queen and wins easily with his superior material.*

4A *White may move his Pawn to the eighth rank and promote to a Queen, even though he already has a Queen on the board. Then, with two Queens against the opponent's single Queen, White can win with ease.*

4B *White may promote his Pawn to a Knight, even though he has two Knights on the board. When White promotes to a Knight, the Black King will be in check and White will win the Queen on his next move.*

HOW THE PAWN CAPTURES
"EN PASSANT"

ON A PREVIOUS page, we explained the Pawn's method of capturing. There is, however, a special type of Pawn capture which happens *occasionally* in a game. When a Pawn advances to a square on the fifth rank of the board, it is permitted a capturing privilege called capturing "en passant" (while passing). This special type of capture is illustrated in the diagrams on the next page.

Diagram 1A shows a White Pawn on the fifth rank. This Pawn controls the two white squares diagonally in front of it; in other words, if either of the two Black Pawns in the diagram moved forward *one square*, the White Pawn could capture it.

In Diagram 1B, one of the Black Pawns has moved forward *two squares*, as it is permitted to do on its first move. In doing so, it has passed through the square on which the White Pawn could have captured it. This gives the White Pawn the right to capture the Black Pawn, *just as though it had moved forward only one square*.

Diagram 1C shows the White Pawn exercising the power of capturing "en passant." The Black Pawn has been captured *while passing*—just as though it had moved only one square.

Capturing "en passant" can only be done with a Pawn on the fifth rank and affects only adverse Pawns on the adjoining files attempting to pass its normal range of capture. The "en passant" capture is optional but the capture must be made immediately or not at all. Thus, in Diagram 1B, if White decides not to capture "en passant" the Black King's Pawn is immune from that method of capture.

1A The White Pawn is on the fifth rank and controls the two white squares diagonally in front of it (K6 and QB6). If either of the Black Pawns advances one square, White can capture it in the ordinary way.

1B One of the Black Pawns has moved two squares, thus passing through a square controlled by the White Pawn. This gives White the right to capture "en passant."

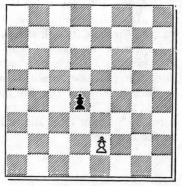

1C The White Pawn has captured "en passant" — while passing. The capture is made just as though the Black Pawn had advanced one square.

2 Another example is shown here. Black's Pawn is on his fifth rank. If White advances his Pawn two squares, Black may capture "en passant" on his next move.

WHEN A CAPTURE is the *only legal move* on the board, the player must make the capture or resign the game. This rule applies to ordinary captures, or to the en passant capture, as illustrated in the positions below.

3A Black has just moved his Pawn two squares forward and is checking the White King. White must capture en passant to get out of check,

3B White has captured en passant. This was the only way in which White could get out of check. Consequently, the capture was forced.

4A Black has just moved his KKt Pawn two squares forward (from Kt2 to Kt4) and now White must capture en passant. He has no legal moves with his King.

4B White has captured en passant. In this case the capture was forced because it was the only legal move at White's disposal.

How GAMES Are DRAWN

A GAME in which neither player can force checkmate is called a draw. Obviously, if all the chessmen are exchanged until the Kings alone are left on the board, the game cannot be won. Similarly, certain endings are automatically drawn because it is *impossible* to checkmate with the available material. Other endings are "technically" drawn because checkmate cannot be forced, even though possible against inferior defense.

There are other special conditions under which games are drawn, as explained in this section.

DRAWN POSITIONS WITHOUT PAWNS

IN DECIDING whether or not an ending can be won, an important consideration is the presence or absence of Pawns on the board. So long as there are any Pawns left, there is always the possibility that one may be queened. Therefore, if you are playing an ending with Pawns on the board, you should continue until a decision is reached.

If all the Pawns are off the board, a player *must be ahead at least a Rook or two minor pieces* (as the Bishops and Knights are called) *to be able to win.* The reason for this can be understood when it is realized that, if everything else is exchanged, a player must be left with at least *one Queen,* or *one Rook,* or *two Bishops,* or *a Bishop and Knight* to be able to force checkmate of a lone King. Final mates with the above pieces are illustrated in diagrams 1 to 4.

Note, however, that it is impossible to checkmate a lone King with *King and Bishop* (diagram 5) or with *King and Knight.* Even a *King and two Knights* cannot force checkmate (diagram 6). In the last case, checkmate is possible only if a blunder is made.

1 Checkmate of a lone King can easily be forced by a King and Queen. The King is driven to the edge of the board and then mated as shown above or in the manner illustrated in diagram 2 with a Queen or Rook.

2 A King and Rook can also force checkmate of a lone King. The typical mating position is shown above. The Black King has been driven to the edge of the board. The Rook checks and the White King blocks any escape.

3 A King and 2 Bishops can compel checkmate. The King is driven into a corner and then mated with the co-operation of all three pieces as illustrated above. One Bishop checks while the other Bishop and the King prevent escape.

4 A King, Bishop and Knight can also force mate, although this conclusion is unusual in actual games. The mating technique is tricky. In the final mate, shown here, the Bishop checks while the Knight and King prevent escape.

5 This position is a draw. In two successive moves the White King will capture the two Pawns—but it is impossible for a King and Bishop to checkmate a lone King.

6 This position is a draw. A King and ONE Knight cannot possibly checkmate a lone King. A King and TWO Knights can checkmate only if a blunder is made by the player with the lone King.

TECHNICALLY DRAWN GAMES

IN COMPLETELY EVEN endings, such as the position of diagram 1, it is customary for players to agree to a draw, as only an outright blunder can produce a win. If Pawns cannot be queened and the remaining material is even, there is seldom any reason for continuing the game.

In other endings, the material may be unequal but the advantage insufficient to win. For instance, the position of diagram 2 is an easy draw. Although White is a Pawn ahead, he can never queen the Pawn unless Black co-operates and helps his own defeat. However, the defense in unequal endings is sometimes difficult, as in the case of King and Rook vs. King and Bishop. The player with winning chances against inferior defense may decide to continue the game.

To break a possible impasse and prevent interminable attempts to win drawn games, the rules of chess provide that a game is drawn if 50 moves have been made on each side without checkmate having been given and without any man having been captured or Pawn moved. Needless to say, this rule is seldom invoked except in tournament or match play.

1 In positions like this players agree to a draw. Only an obvious blunder can lose the game.

2 Although White is ahead in material, Black can easily draw this ending. White cannot queen the Pawn.

DRAW BY STALEMATE

WE HAVE LEARNED that checkmate is the victorious conclusion of a game. The King is checkmated when he is in *check and cannot get out of check.*

However, the player in a winning position must be careful to avoid "stalemating" his opponent. A stalemate occurs when the player who is supposed to move has, in fact, *no legal moves* and his King is *not in check.*

When a stalemate position is reached, the game is automatically drawn.

The following diagrams show typical stalemates. Note that, in each case, the player on the move is unable to make a legal move with any of his men and that his King is *not* in check. He cannot move his King without going into check and he cannot move any of his remaining men because they are blocked or "pinned."

Stalemate usually occurs in the endgame when most of the pieces are off the board. Sometimes the stalemate cannot be avoided but frequently a player with a lost game will out-maneuver his opponent and force a stalemate, thus obtaining a draw. Diagrams 8A, 8B and 8C illustrate the use of the stalemate idea in saving an otherwise lost game.

1 It is Black's turn to move, but his King cannot move without going into check. As he is not in check and has no legal moves left, he is stalemate and the game is drawn.

2 Black, whose turn it is to move, is unable to make a legal move and his King is not in check. He is therefore stalemate and the game is drawn.

3 It is Black's turn to move. His King is not in check but the King cannot move without going into check. The black squares are attacked by the Pawn, the white squares by the White King. A stalemate.

4 It is White's turn to move. His Knight cannot move, his Pawns are blocked and his King cannot move without going into check. The position is a draw by stalemate.

5 White to play, but he has no legal moves and his King is not in check. His Knight and Pawn are blocked. His Rook cannot move without exposing his King to check by the Black Queen. His King cannot move without going into check. A stalemate.

6 White to play but he is stalemate. Two of his Pawns are blocked; the third cannot move as the King would be exposed to check. The Bishop is blocked and the Knight cannot move (even though this would check the Black King) as any move by the Knight would be illegal. The King itself cannot move.

7 Black has just made a capture with his Queen, but in doing so has stalemated White. As White's King is not in check and he has no legal moves, the game is drawn by stalemate.

8A In this position, White is in danger of losing the game. Black is a Queen and Pawn ahead which is more than sufficient to force a win in ordinary circumstances.

8B But White finds an ingenious way of saving the game. He has checked the Black King with his Rook, apparently giving away this piece as Black can just capture it.

8C Black has captured the checking Rook with his own Rook (the only way he could get out of check) and now White has no legal moves. He has saved the game by forcing stalemate.

DRAW BY PERPETUAL CHECK

Black draws by perpetual check. Note that a Rook, turned upside down, is used to represent a second Queen.

BECAUSE OF the possibility of stalemate, many "lost" endings are continued. The player on the losing end hopes that a mistake will be made, enabling him to draw the game by stalemate.

There is another way in which an otherwise lost game can be rescued. If a player proves that he can subject his opponent's King to an *endless series of checks*, the game is drawn. This method is called "drawing by perpetual check" and can take place at any stage of the game.

An example of perpetual check is given in the picture on this page. Here White has queened a Pawn and now has *two Queens* on the board. (Note: chessplayers use a Rook turned upside down to represent a second Queen.) Of course White has sufficient material advantage to win but Black draws by perpetual check.

In the position shown, the White King is in check and the only way to get out of check is by interposing one of the Queens. Black then checks by moving to another corner of the triangle in the picture, the actual corner depending on which Queen has been interposed. Again White must interpose one of his Queens and Black then checks by moving to the third corner of the triangle, or by returning to the position in the photo. This procedure could continue indefinitely and White cannot prevent the endless series of checks.

Other examples of perpetual check are given in diagrams 1 and 2.

1 White is a Rook behind and is threatened with immediate checkmate. He saves the game by perpetual check. The White Rook can check indefinitely on the two squares in front of the Black King.

2 Here Black's advantage in material would be overwhelming but White draws by perpetual check. The White Queen can check indefinitely on the 7th and 8th squares of the King-Bishop's file.

DRAW BY REPETITION

To TAKE CARE of situations in which both players keep *repeating the same moves*, the rules of chess specify that a game is drawn if the same position is repeated three times.

It sometimes happens that equality can only be maintained by repetition of this nature. Each player keeps moving the same piece back and forth. If the game is to continue, one of the players must change the position by making a different move; otherwise the game is drawn after the third repetition.

PART TWO

Basic Principles

RELATIVE VALUES OF THE CHESSMEN

MAJOR PIECES

	Value
Queen	9
Rook	5

MINOR PIECES

Bishop	3
Knight	3

PAWN 1

THROUGHOUT a chess game the men are constantly being exchanged. As the pieces are unequal in value, the player must be able to decide whether exchanges are an "even swap" or whether they are profitable or unprofitable. (An "exchange" is a capture and recapture. However, this term usually signifies an *even* exchange.)

Obviously, the Queen is much more valuable than a Rook because the Queen can move in twice as many directions as the Rook. Similarly, the Rook is more valuable than a Bishop or Knight because of its long-range attack on white and black squares.

The composite photo above shows how the different types of chessmen would appear *if their sizes corresponded with their "exchanging values."* The King is not included as he cannot be exchanged.

Considering the Pawn as the unit of value, a Queen is worth 9 units, a Rook is worth 5 units and a Bishop or Knight is worth

95

3 units. The Queen and Rooks are known as the "major pieces" while the Bishops and Knights are called "minor pieces." (Although the general term "pieces" is often used when referring to all the chessmen, the same term more specifically refers to the major and minor pieces, in contradistinction to the Pawns.)

Note how the Queen towers above all the other men. The ability to move and capture in all directions makes the Queen the most valuable of all the chessmen. In the center of an open board, the Queen controls no less than 27 squares. No other piece has such power.

If you exchange Queens with your opponent, you are making an even exchange; but if you give up your Queen for *any other man* you are definitely not getting full value and the sacrifice should cost you the game, unless it enables you to checkmate.

Occasionally, the Queen can be exchanged for *two Rooks* and this is an approximately even swap. In fact, two Rooks are worth about a Pawn more than a Queen. There are other combinations of pieces and Pawns roughly equivalent in value to a Queen (three minor pieces plus Pawn; or Rook plus minor piece plus Pawn) but these exchanges are exceptional. The beginner should make sure of getting nothing less than his opponent's Queen for his own Queen and leave the other combinations to more advanced players, unless they are forced upon him.

The Rook is next in value to the Queen. In any position on an open board a Rook controls 14 white and black squares. A Rook is worth a Bishop and 2 Pawns, or a Knight and 2 Pawns; but in actual practice, the Rook is seldom exchanged for anything except the opponent's Rook. However, if you can capture *two* of your opponent's minor pieces for one of your Rooks, do not hesitate to make the exchange. A Bishop and Knight (or 2 Bishops, or 2 Knights) are worth much more than one Rook.

The Bishop and Knight are approximately equal in exchanging value. Offhand, the Bishop may seem stronger than the Knight. It is true that the Bishop has a longer range and controls more squares (maximum: Bishop 13, Knight 8) but the Bishop is *confined to squares of one color* and this limitation reduces its value to the equivalent of a Knight. However, two Bishops, controlling both white and black squares, are considered stronger than two Knights.

A Bishop or Knight is worth 3 Pawns, but in practice a minor piece is generally exchanged for another minor piece. *Two* minor pieces are equal to a Rook plus 2 Pawns and *three* minor pieces are equal to two Rooks—but such exchanges are unusual. If you capture a Rook with one of your minor pieces you are making a profit; the transaction is called "winning the exchange."

As the Pawn controls only two squares, its capturing power is limited and it is the least valuable of the chessmen, *so far as exchanges are concerned.* As pointed out previously, however, the general worth of the Pawn should not be underrated. Its potential value for the ending is extremely important as each Pawn is a possible Queen. Moreover, its comparatively low exchanging value makes it an effective unit for both attack and defense. Although the Pawn has a low exchanging value, this does not mean that Pawns can be given away with impunity.

RULE FOR EXCHANGING

Always get your money's worth, or better, when making exchanges.

Remember the picture of the ENORMOUS QUEEN, the BIG ROOK, the SMALL KNIGHT AND BISHOP, the TINY PAWN and be guided accordingly.

If you exchange Queen for Queen, Rook for Rook, Bishop or Knight for Bishop or Knight, Pawn for Pawn, the result is equal. But if you give up a piece for a less valuable piece, or if you give up any minor or major piece for a Pawn, you will probably lose the game.

Every rule has exceptions. These exceptions do not prove the rule unsound. They merely demonstrate that other factors have entered into the situation and permit the rule to be broken.

Chess is a charming and imaginative game because the relative values of the men are not static but are influenced by the positions occurring on the board. The beautiful combinations, the brilliant and artistic conceptions created with chessmen, are brought about by sacrifices of material, usually culminating in checkmate. A Queen may be given up to allow a meek little Pawn to administer a crushing blow. A Knight may wreak havoc where a Rook might be helpless. In all such cases, material is deliberately sacrificed with a greater advantage in view.

The positional factors which influence the values of the men will be explained later. Meantime, the learner should avoid sacrifices of material unless he clearly sees a continuation which forces checkmate or the regain of material sacrificed. Such continuations must leave the opponent no options, must not depend upon his co-operation.

Some examples of even and uneven exchanges are given on the following pages. When reading the explanations under the diagrams, note the style in which the chess notation is written. When moves are recorded one after the other (not tabulated) a comma is placed after each White move and a semicolon after each Black move.

EXAMPLES OF EXCHANGES

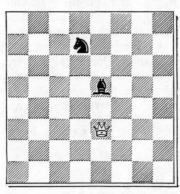

1 An even exchange. If White captures the Bishop, Black can recapture with the Knight. This exchange, and the exchanges in the following diagrams, should be pictured mentally. In chess notation, the above exchange would be written: 1 BxB, KtxB (Bishop takes Bishop, Knight takes Bishop).

2 An uneven exchange. If the Queen captures the Bishop, the Knight recaptures the Queen. White would lose heavily by this transaction as the Queen is worth more than three minor pieces. This exchange would be recorded as 1 QxB??, KtxQ. The two question marks indicate that White's move is a blunder.

3 White can win a piece because the Black Bishop is attacked twice, defended once, and White can start by playing BxB (Bishop takes Bishop). If Black recaptures, White plays QxKt (Queen takes Knight). In chess notation, the entire transaction would be written: 1 BxB, KtxB; 2 QxKt. But White must not play 1 QxB??, KtxQ; 2 BxKt, losing his Queen for two minor pieces.

4 Now the Black Bishop is attacked twice, defended twice, so White cannot gain any material advantage. White can exchange Bishops (BxB, KtxB) but if he continues with QxKt the Pawn will recapture his Queen which would be disastrous. Follow the exchanges in chess notation: 1 BxB, KtxB; 2 QxKt??, PxQ. One of the main functions of a Pawn is to guard pieces in this manner.

5 The Black Bishop is attacked twice, defended only once, but White cannot win material advantage because the first capture would be with the Queen. Thus, if 1 QxB??, KtxQ; 2 RxKt, White has exchanged his Queen for a Bishop and Knight—a losing transaction.

6 Similar to the position of diagram 5, but now White can gain a material advantage because the Rook and Queen are transposed. He can exchange his Rook for two minor pieces by playing 1 RxB, KtxR; 2 QxKt. The Bishop and Knight are worth more than the Rook.

7 White to play. The Black Knight is attacked 3 times, defended only twice, but White cannot win material because the defending units are less valuable than the attacking pieces. White can exchange Knights, but after 1 KtxKt, PxKt, he must not play 2 RxP?, BxR; 3 RxB. Or after 1 Ktx Kt, BxKt (instead of PxKt), he must not play 2 RxB?, PxR; 3 RxP. In either case he wins a Pawn but loses the exchange (R for B).

8 White to play. Similar to position 7, but now White can win a Pawn because he can make the second capture with a minor piece. Thus, after 1 KtxKt, PxKt; 2 BxP, White has won a Pawn and if Black continues 2...BxB; 3 RxB is an even exchange. Or if 1 KtxKt, BxKt; 2 BxB, PxB; 3 RxP, again winning a Pawn. As explained under diagram 7, White must not make the first or second capture with his Rook.

9 White to play. Black's QP is attacked 4 times, guarded only twice, but White cannot win material as the attacking pieces are more valuable than the defenders. White can play 1 PxP but after 1 ... PxP or 1 ... KtxP he must not capture the Pawn or Kt.

10 White to play. Now White can win a Pawn as he can make the second capture with a minor piece. After 1 PxP, PxP; 2 KtxP, White has won a Pawn and if 2 ... KtxKt; 3 RxKt is an even exchange. Or if 1 PxP, KtxP; 2 KtxKt, PxKt; 3 RxP

NOTE THAT captures and recaptures are usually made *in the order represented by the values of the attacking or defending units.* Thus, the first capture may be made with a Pawn, the second with a minor piece, the third with a Rook or Queen. Similarly, the defender recaptures with a Pawn, then a minor piece, etc. This is by no means a rigid rule applying to all situations, but the order in which captures or recaptures *can* be made must always be borne in mind.

Note, too, that the resulting gain or loss of material after a series of exchanges is determined by both the *quantity and quality* of the attacking and defending units. Both factors must be considered.

To determine whether you can win material (or whether you are threatened with the loss of material), always count the number of *attacking* units and the number of *defending* units. If the defense is *outnumbered*, the attacking player can "win" one of the opponent's men. For instance, he can capture two men in exchange for one of his own, or he can capture three men in exchange for two of his own. However, the comparative *quality* of the exchanged units decides whether the transaction is favorable or otherwise. To gain material advantage, the captured men must be worth more than the men that have been given up to capture them.

SUPERIOR FORCE SHOULD WIN

THE most important factor in winning a game of chess is *superiority in material*. At the beginning of the game, the opposing forces are equal. Each player has the same number of men, the same quality of material. But if, during the course of the game, one player gains material (for instance, by capturing an unprotected piece, or by making a profitable exchange, or by accepting a meaningless sacrifice) the forces are no longer equal and *the player who is ahead in material should win the game.*

This is one of the fundamental principles of chess. The purpose of most attacks is to gain material at the expense of the opponent. As the chessmen have different values, material superiority is measured in quality as well as quantity. A player who "wins the exchange" by giving up a Knight or Bishop to capture a Rook is ahead in material, even though he has the same number of men as his opponent.

Even the comparatively insignificant gain of one Pawn may be sufficient to win. By holding this advantage throughout the game and by exchanging the remaining material, the player who is a Pawn up may be able to reach an ending in which his extra Pawn can be promoted to a Queen. As we have seen, a Queen is sufficient to force checkmate.

The gain of more important material than a Pawn gives an overwhelming advantage to the superior force. A player who is a Rook or Queen ahead can usually end the game quickly with an immediate attack on the King. The gain of a minor piece (Bishop or Knight) requires a certain knowledge of technique to force a win but, in a contest between experienced players, the outcome should never be in doubt. In such cases, the player who is a piece up may use his superior force to win more material, or he may decide to exchange most of the remaining men and reach an ending in which his advantage is comparatively greater, enabling him to queen a Pawn and finish the game in short order.

Contests between strong players usually end in immediate resignation if a minor or major piece is lost without compensation and if there is no chance of launching an attack to regain material, checkmate the King, or draw by perpetual check. It is recognized that the player who is a piece up can force a win, that it is merely a matter of technique, even though it may take some time.

In contests between inexperienced players, however, the loss of a piece may be a mere incident in the game. The tide of battle may sway from one side to the other. The players enjoy themselves thoroughly as they fight it out to the bitter end. Even against hopeless odds, resignation is never contemplated—and rightly so, as the other fellow is quite capable of blundering away his advantage.

It is also true that a strong player can "give odds" to a weak opponent and win the game. For instance, in a recent "rapid transit" (ten seconds a move) tourney, chessmaster

I. A. Horowitz actually gave odds of a Queen, Rook, Bishop and Knight to one of his opponents—and won!

Therefore, when we say that material superiority should win, it will be realized that we are stating a principle which applies, in practice, to games between experienced players of approximately equal strength. The fundamental nature of the principle, however, should not be overlooked by the learner if he wishes to graduate from the beginner class.

RULES FOR LEARNERS

You CANNOT expect to win chess games by giving away material to your opponent! Conserve your pieces and pawns—they are your "material." This does not mean that you should be afraid to make exchanges. You and your opponent must make exchanges, or there would be no game. But get your money's worth when making or allowing exchanges—and try to avoid the outright loss of material.

Take a good look at the square to which you intend to move one of your minor or major pieces and make sure that there are no Pawns attacking the square—remembering the Pawn's V-shaped capture. Look at your opponent's other pieces—his Queen, Rooks, Bishops, and Knights—and see if they are attacking the square to which you intend to move. If the square is attacked, do you want him to take your piece? Will you be able to recapture and will the exchange be even or profitable? Is he attacking the square with 2 or more men—and if so, are you defending the square with the same number of men? These are some of the things you should consider before making a move.

At first, when you are unfamiliar with the chessboard, you will lose material by oversights. To use the international chess expression, you will put or leave pieces "en prise" (pronounced *awng preeze*) which means "on take" without compensation. As you gain experience, you will overcome this fault, common to all beginners and not unknown among masters.

Don't take moves back. Suffer the consequences of your mistakes and you will learn to avoid them. The rules of chess specify that if a player touches one of his own men he must move it, and if he touches one of his opponent's men he must capture it, provided the move or capture is legal. (If illegal, there is no penalty.) If he merely wants to adjust the position of a man (or men) he must announce this intention, using the international expression "J'adoube" (meaning: I · adjust. Pronounced *Zhah-doob*).

HOW TO MEET CAPTURING THREATS

DURING A GAME of chess, the players are constantly "threatening" to capture each other's men. Almost every move attacks something or defends an opponent's threat.

At all times, you must be on guard against these threats. You must not allow your opponent to capture one of your men without being able to capture an *equally valuable* man in return. In other words, you must avoid the loss of material.

One of the best methods of protecting yourself from loss is to guard your exposed pieces with Pawns. Then, if one of them is captured by an enemy piece, your Pawn can recapture. As a rule, it is a mistake to leave a piece too long in an exposed position without being guarded by a Pawn. *An unguarded piece is a weakness in your position.* It may be temporarily safe, but it has to be continually watched and you may lose the piece by an oversight or by a tactical maneuver on the part of your opponent. (For instance, he may check your King and simultaneously attack your unguarded piece.)

An exposed piece can also be guarded by another piece, instead of by a Pawn. In some positions this is perfectly satisfactory, but on many occasions it is a mistake to tie one piece down to the defense of another. Sometimes it is unsafe—and it restricts the mobility of the defending piece. As a rule, you should free your pieces from purely defensive roles. Pawns are the best defenders.

If your opponent attacks one of your men, *there are various ways of meeting the threat of capture.* Don't feel that you must move the attacked man. Very often it is better to allow the capture, provided you can recapture. However, if you don't want him to exchange, there are other things you can do. For your guidance, we list the various methods below. One or more of these resources should be available, the choice of method being a matter of judgment.

(a) If not already protected, guard the attacked man and permit an exchange, provided the exchange is even or in your favor. A Pawn is usually the best guard.

(b) Move your attacked man to a vacant square where it is protected or free from attack.

(c) Capture the attacking unit, either with the man under attack or with another of your men.

(d) Capture something else with your attacked man.

(e) Prevent the capture by interposing another man. Bear in mind that this may permit capture of the interposed unit.

(f) Pin the attacking unit so that the threatened capture becomes illegal or unprofitable.

(g) Counter-attack by capturing elsewhere on the board, or by checking the opponent's King, or by making a threat of your own which is at least as dangerous as your opponent's threat.

Some examples of the use of these methods are given on the next two pages.

1 White to play. Black is threatening to capture the unprotected Pawn. There are three ways in which White can meet this threat. He can guard the attacked Pawn with his other Pawn, permitting an exchange; or he can immediately capture the attacking Pawn; or he can move his attacked Pawn forward one square.

2 White to play. Black is threatening to capture a Bishop with his Pawn. White must not permit this capture. He has three ways of meeting the threat. He can play BxB; or he can move his Bishop back one square, allowing Black to exchange; or he can pin the attacking Pawn by moving his Rook one square to the left.

3 White to play. Black is threatening to capture the unprotected Bishop. White has four ways of meeting the threat. He can guard the Bishop with a Pawn; or he can capture the Black Bishop; or he can move his Bishop out of the line of attack; or he can prevent the capture by interposing a Pawn, playing 1 P–B5.

4 White to play. Black has a major threat which cannot be met by ordinary means. He threatens to capture White's Queen with his Bishop and the Queen is pinned, cannot move away. Counter-attack is the only way to avoid serious loss. White equalizes with 1 B–Q5ch, Q–K3 (forced); 2 BxQch, RxB; 3 QxB, PxQ.

5 White to play. Black is threatening to win a piece as White's Rook (at K1) is attacked twice, defended once. To guard the Rook again would not do, as Black would win the exchange with 1 ... KtxR. White can meet the threat by capturing BxKt or RxR; or he can move the attacked Rook one square to the right.

6 White to play. Black's threat is QxQ. White can choose one of four ways to meet this threat. He can capture the Black Queen; or move his own Queen out of the line of attack; or he can interpose his Rook, playing 1 R–Q7; or he can guard and permit the exchange of Queens by moving his Rook one square to the left, playing 1 R–B1.

7 Black to play. White is attacking the Kt with four pieces and threatens to win a Pawn after BxKt etc. Black must choose his reply with care. If he moves his Kt he loses his Rook. If he plays R (at K1) to QB1, White wins the exchange with Kt–Q5. Black's best reply is P–K5, interposing a Pawn and attacking the Bishop.

8 Black to play. White is threatening RxB and is also attacking the QKtP with Rook and Queen. No ordinary methods will meet these two threats—but Black sees a way to counter-attack. He plays 1 ... R–B6! attacking White's Queen. Then follows 2 PxR, BxPch; 3 K–Kt2, BxR, recovering the sacrificed piece and winning a Pawn.

Threats and Counter-threats

WE HAVE SEEN that there are various ways of meeting the threat of capture and this choice of method is one of the most interesting aspects of chess. Throughout the entire game, the players attack, defend, or counter-attack. Each threat must be carefully considered and answered in the best way. If a threat is ignored, or overlooked, the player who wins material immediately gains a great advantage and should win the game.

The threats and counter-threats start almost with the opening move. As each player brings out a piece, he usually threatens to win material or guards one of his units which has been threatened by the opponent. To illustrate this point, the following diagrams depict the opening moves of a typical chess game. Note how each move either threatens or defends. Usually there is a choice of method in answering the threats. Sometimes there are two or three capturing threats and the player must see that all his pieces are defended so that he will not lose material.

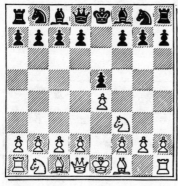

1 This game has begun with the moves 1 P–K4, P–K4; 2 Kt–KB3. White is now threatening to capture Black's Pawn. The Pawn is unprotected so Black must meet this threat or lose material. Black can counter-attack by playing Kt–KB3 or he can guard the Pawn.

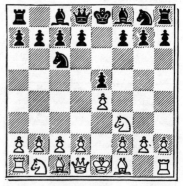

2 Black has played 2 ... Kt–QB3. This defends the threatened Pawn. If White, on his next move, were to play KtxP, Black would capture the Knight, gaining a Knight for a Pawn. The players must visualize these captures and recaptures without touching the pieces.

3 Now White has played 3 P–Q4.

With this move he attacks the Black Pawn a second time. It is attacked twice, defended once. Hence, White threatens to win a Pawn. Black now considers the various ways of meeting this new threat before making his move.

4 Black has played 3 ... PxP capturing one of the attacking men with the threatened Pawn itself. Refer again to diagram 3 and note that Black had other ways of meeting the threat. He could have defended the Pawn a second time or captured with the Knight—but he chose best.

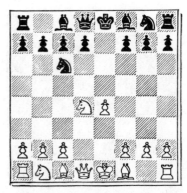

5 White has played 4 KtxP, completing the exchange of Pawns, and now it is Black's turn to move. Black sees that White is threatening to capture his Knight, but the threat is not serious as the Black Knight is protected by 2 Pawns. His material is safe. Black could exchange Knights himself but nothing would be gained, so he develops a piece.

6 Black has played 4 ... Kt–B3 bringing out his other Kt. It is White's turn and he notes that Black is now threatening two captures (KtxKt and KtxP). The White Knight is guarded by the Queen but the Pawn is unprotected. To avoid the loss of material, White must move or guard his threatened Pawn —or answer Black's threat with a counter-attack (KtxKt).

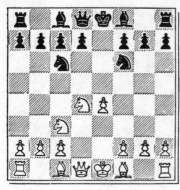

7 White has played 5 Kt–QB3 bringing out his Queen–Kt and defending his Pawn. In this way he meets Black's threat and at the same time mobilizes a piece. Now it is Black's move and he sees that White has made no new threats, that his material is all safe. He decides to develop a piece with a new threat of his own.

8 Black has played 5...B–Kt5. With this move he pins White's Queen–Knight. Any move by this Kt would now be illegal as the King would be exposed to check. Hence, the Knight no longer defends the threatened Pawn. Black threatens KtxP and White's Knight cannot recapture. White must meet this threat immediately.

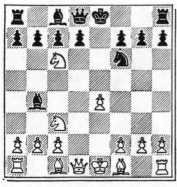

9 White has played 6 KtxKt. See diagram 8 and note that Black was threatening three captures but the main threat was KtxP. White has now answered this dangerous threat with a counter-attack. Black's Knight has been captured and his Queen is attacked.

10 Black has played 6...KtPxKt and White has played 7 B–Q3. Black was forced to answer the counter-attack and now his two remaining threats are defended. Only a few moves have been played but enough to show that the fighting begins early in the game.

What Does He Threaten?

MOST BEGINNERS are so busy thinking up their own moves and concentrating on their own plans that they pay little or no attention to what the opponent is doing and soon find themselves checkmated or in a hopeless position.

The method of overcoming this fault is comparatively easy—if you adhere to it. Each time your opponent makes a move, *forget your own plans for a moment and concentrate on HIS move.* Ask yourself this question: *"What does he threaten?"* All strong players follow this procedure and avoid trouble. Emulate their example and your game will rapidly improve. The procedure may be summarized as follows:

Your opponent makes a move. *Look at the piece he just moved.* Dismiss other thoughts and plans from your mind. What does he threaten? Why did he move this piece? In its new position, is the piece attacking one of your men? Can you permit him to capture, or is the attacking piece less valuable than your own man? If he threatens to capture a man of equal or lower value, is your man protected? Will you be able to recapture?

Then look at his *other* pieces. Is he concentrating his fire? Are two or more of his pieces now attacking one of your men? If so, will you lose material if he captures twice (or several times) on the same square?

When he moved his piece, did he unmask an attack by *another* of his men? Look at his Rooks, Bishops and Queen, even if they are still on his first rank and far from the scene of action. Has an attack by one of these pieces been released by the move he just made?

Try to discover your opponent's intention or plan of attack, if any. Is there a secondary or once-removed threat? For instance, on his *next* move will he be able to win material in any way? Will he be able to check your King and will that be dangerous? Did his move "pin" one of your men and will the follow-up cost you material?

If you discover that your opponent's move threatens you with the *loss of material* you must do something about this threat immediately.

Under the heading "How to Meet Capturing Threats" we outlined the various methods of answering such a threat. When the threatened capture would cost you material (quantitatively or qualitatively) you must take action. Select the method you believe best in the circumstances. Defend, interpose, move away, capture, pin the attacker or counter-attack—but do *not* permit your opponent to win material.

Illustrative Game

ON THIS and the following pages we present a move-by-move description of a game between two experts. The game was played between Rafael Blanco and Abraham Kupchik at Havana in 1913.

This game will be used to illustrate the necessity of examining your opponent's threats before making a move. You can follow the game without using a set of chessmen as the position after each move is pictured in the diagrams. The captions explain the moves as they are made.

Although this is a record of an actual game, we ask you to regard yourself as the player of the white forces. With your permission, we will play over this game together, as though we were members of a consultation team. The captions are written with this idea in mind.

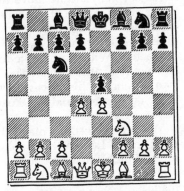

1 The game has begun with the opening moves 1 P–K4, P–K4; 2 Kt–KB3, Kt–QB3. We are playing White and it is our turn to move. Before considering possible plays, we first ask: "What does our opponent threaten?" We see that he has no threats so proceed to develop.

2 As White, we have played P–Q4. We had other good moves at our disposal, such as B–Kt5, or B–B4 or Kt–B3. The move we made threatens to win a Pawn. We are attacking Black's advanced Pawn twice and it is defended only once. Black must meet this threat or lose a Pawn.

3 Black has played PxP and again it is our move. What does he threaten? Well, he is not threatening to capture anything but he has just taken one of our Pawns and if we don't recapture we will have lost material. We have two ways of recapturing but only one is playable.

4 We have played KtxP and Black has played B–B4. Again it is our turn. What does he threaten? He threatens to win our Knight! He is attacking it with two pieces (Bishop and Kt) and it is guarded only by our Queen. We must answer this threat at once—by defending, moving away, or capturing.

5 We decided to guard our threatened Knight with another piece and have played B–K3. But now Black has played Q–B3. What does he threaten? He again threatens to win our Knight! His last move brought a third piece into the fray and he is now attacking the Knight three times. Our defense is outnumbered 3 to 2. Our next move must meet this threat.

6 We have played P–QB3 and this Pawn guards the Kt. Our piece is attacked 3 times and defended 3 times, so it is safe. Now it is Black's move and he can exchange pieces, if he wishes, but he cannot win any material. If he plays KtxKt or BxKt we will recapture with our Pawn and the Pawn will then be safe as Black would lose material if he captured it.

7 Black has played KKt–K2. (Note we must specify King–Knight to K2 as Black's other Knight can also go to this square.) It is our turn to move and the first question is: What does he threaten? We see that Black has made no new threat. He decided to avoid exchanges and just continue his development.

8 So we have played B–K2, developing another piece and preparing to safeguard our King by castling. Black has replied by playing P–Q4. It is again our move. What did Black threaten when he played P–Q4? He attacked our KP and threatens to win a Pawn. We must postpone castling and answer this threat.

9 Our choice of replies was limited. We could not move the Pawn without losing it—and to defend the Pawn would have been awkward and unnecessary. The simplest and best way to answer Black's threat was to capture his attacking Pawn. As shown here, we have played PxP and now our Pawn attacks his Kt.

10 Black has played KtxP, completing the exchange of Pawns. Are there any new threats? Look at the piece he just moved. What does it threaten? We can see that the Knight is now attacking our Bishop and one of our Pawns. Can we afford to let him capture the Bishop? Is this not needed for defense?

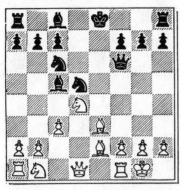

11 We have decided that Black's threats were not dangerous and we have continued our development by castling. The Pawn and Bishop attacked by Black's Kt are both guarded. Black cannot play KtxP without loss and if he plays KtxB, we can play PxKt. Then the recapturing Pawn will take the Bishop's place and guard our Knight.

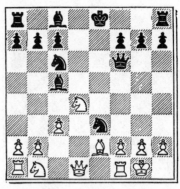

12 Black has played KtxB. He has removed our Bishop from the board and his Knight now attacks our Queen and Rook. There is only one thing to do here. We must recapture immediately. As a rule, recaptures must be made at once, to avoid material loss. Note that when we play PxKt our Rook will be attacking Black's Queen on the open file.

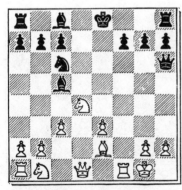

13 We have played PxKt and Black has moved his Queen to R3. What does he threaten? We must not overlook any threats merely because Black was forced to move his Queen. In its new position, is the Queen threatening anything? Yes, our unprotected KP is now attacked. We must answer this threat by moving the Pawn or guarding it.

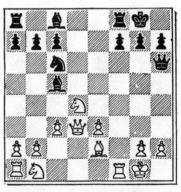

14 We have played Q–Q3, protecting the attacked Pawn, and Black has castled. Our Queen move answered Black's threat and at the same time placed our Queen on a more commanding square. Note how threats are often met by developing pieces on active squares. Are there any new threats? None. All our material is safe.

15 As Black did not threaten anything when he castled we have continued our mobilization by playing Kt–Q2 and Black has played B–Q3. Why did he change the position of this Bishop? Looking down the Bishop's diagonal, we find that our KRP is the target! He is threatening BxPch or QxPch. Quick! Our King is in danger!

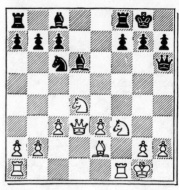

16 We have come to the defense of our King by playing Kt (at Q2) to B3. Our KRP is attacked twice (by Black's Queen and Bishop) but is now guarded twice (by our Knight and King) so we are safe for the time being. But we must be careful. Black is assaulting our King's position and we must concentrate on defense.

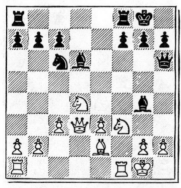

17 Black has played B–KKt5. What does he threaten now? This new piece is threatening to capture our Knight and this Kt is needed to defend our KRP. However, if he plays BxKt we can recapture KtxB and our other Kt will guard the KRP. But suppose he plays Knight takes Knight first: how can we meet this threat?

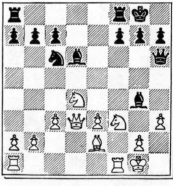

18 We have played P–KR3, attacking Black's Bishop, because his real threat (in position 17) was KtxKt. To protect our King we would have been forced to recapture KPxKt and then he could play Bx Kt, followed by BxPch, at least winning a Pawn. But our Pawn move has met this threat. If he now plays KtxKt, we can recapture KtxKt.

116

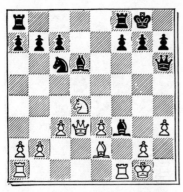

19 Black realized that we had successfully anticipated his threats and that he would gain nothing by playing KtxKt. Instead, he has captured BxKt. Now we need not recapture with our Knight because our KRP is safe, having moved out of the range of fire. We must recapture, but we can do so with our Rook or Bishop.

20 We have recaptured with our Bishop (BxB) and Black has played Kt–K4. Look at the piece he has just moved. What does he threaten? The answer is obvious. His Knight now attacks our Queen and Bishop! We must meet this threat immediately and as we cannot capture the attacking Knight, we must move our Queen.

21 We have moved our Queen to K4 and Black has played QR–K1. Why did he move this Rook? His main threat is to play KtxBch, when his Rook will be attacking our Queen. After we recapture QxKt he will play QxPch, winning a Pawn and forcing exchange of Queens, with good chances of winning the game. How shall we answer?

22 By a counter-attack! We have played Kt–B5 and our Knight attacked Black's Queen and Bishop. At the same time, the Knight guards our vulnerable KP, defending the threat. Black has moved his attacked Queen to K3. Any new threats? Not immediate, but we must remember that our Queen is not very safe.

23 We have played KtxB. This was another reason for our last move. We attacked his Queen to answer his threats and to gain time for this capture. His Bishop was dangerous. Our King is vulnerable along black square diagonals. He had possible mating threats with his Queen and Bishop. By removing his Bishop we have eliminated this danger.

24 Black has recaptured QxKt. Any new threats? His Queen is not attacking anything but he still threatens KtxBch, with a disclosed attack on our Queen. However, the sting has been taken out of this threat now as our KP is temporarily safe. But this "isolated" Pawn is a weakness. Unprotected by other Pawns, it is difficult to defend.

25 Our Queen was in an uncomfortable position, subject to attack, so we decided to move it. We have played QxP. Black's Pawn was unprotected and we are now ahead in material. We are also attacking Black's QRP which is unguarded. We begin to develop a plan which may enable us to win the game.

26 Black has replied by playing Kt–B5. By making this move, he now attacks our unprotected KP twice (with Kt and R) and threatens to win the Pawn, recovering his lost material. We cannot defend our Pawn against this double attack; and if we advance the Pawn Black will play Q–B4ch, guarding his QRP.

27 We have played QxRP and Black has captured KtxKP. We decided it was better to let our KP go and maintain our advantage by capturing another Black Pawn. We are still one Pawn ahead and it is our turn to move. What does Black threaten? His Knight is attacking our Rook and he threatens to win the exchange.

28 We have moved our attacked Rook to K1 and Black has returned his Kt to B5. Are there any threats we must take care of? We see that Black can play RxR, but our Rook is guarded; if he captures, we can recapture with our other Rook. How about his Knight, the piece he just moved? Yes, he threatens to capture our unguarded QKtP.

29 What's this? We have played Q–Q4. Are we not going to protect that Pawn? So far, we have answered all Black's threats but now we are letting him take a Pawn. Why? Because the time has come to capitalize on the advantage of a "passed Pawn." We are going to try to win the game by advancing our unopposed QRP to the 8th rank.

30 Black has played KtxP and we have played QxQ. Our QKtP was not essential to the execution of our winning idea. Our plan is to exchange as many of the remaining pieces as possible to forestall any counter-attacks. Although we are no longer ahead in material, our passed Pawn (unopposed by enemy Pawns) will decide the issue.

31 Black has recaptured PxQ and we have played RxR. Pursuing our plan, we continue to liquidate everything in sight. The less men there are on the board, the more dangerous our passed Pawn will become when we start advancing it. By exchanging pieces we also reduce the possibility of any counterplay by Black.

32 Black has recaptured RxR and we have started our passed Pawn on its way by playing P–QR4. If possible, we are going to advance this Pawn to the 8th rank. This threat may cost Black a piece or win the game in other ways. Note that our Bishop controls the queening square (QR8) and that our Rook protects the Pawn.

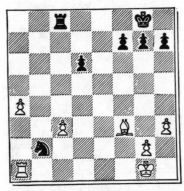

33 Black has played R–QB1. What does he threaten? Well, he threatens RxP, but we are not going to pay any attention to his threats now unless they are dangerous. We are on the offensive and can afford to ignore Black's minor threats. Note that Black could have played KtxP but this would have cost him a piece.

34 We have advanced the QRP another square forward and Black has played Kt–B5. He could not afford to take our QBP with his Rook. Our passed Pawn is becoming more and more threatening. He is scurrying back with his Knight to use this piece for defense. He is trying to prevent our Pawn from reaching the 8th rank.

35 *On goes the Pawn! We have played P–R6 and the threatening Pawn stands on the 6th rank. Black has played Kt–Kt3 and his Knight defends the queening square. If we play P–R7 and P–R8 he intends to sacrifice his Kt for our promoted Pawn. This material gain would be sufficient to win the game eventually, but there is a much quicker way.*

36 *We have played R–Kt1 attacking the Knight. By analyzing a few moves ahead we can see a forced win which will end the game much sooner than permitting Black to sacrifice his Knight. Black must now move his Knight. If he guards it with R–Kt1 we will play P–R7 which wins a piece (either the Rook or Kt) and retains the passed Pawn.*

37 *Black had no option. He was forced to move his Kt. He has played it to R1 (our QR8). Now he is attempting to block our passed Pawn. This is the customary defensive technique used by a player who is trying to prevent a passed Pawn from queening. He blocks the progress of the Pawn with a piece.*

38 *We have removed the block by playing BxKt. But how does this accomplish anything? Obviously, Black will recapture RxB and then his Rook will not only be blocking our passed Pawn but will also be threatening to capture it. Then, if we just defend the Pawn by playing R–R1 we will be unable to make further progress.*

121

39 As we expected, Black has re- captured RxB, but instead of defending our Pawn, we have played P–R7! This is the winning move and at this point Black resigns be- cause he is unable to meet our threats. No matter what he does, he either gets mated or must permit us to make a new Queen. The follow- ing three diagrams explain why he resigned.

39A In the position of the pre- vious diagram (39) White was threatening R–Kt8ch which would force Black to capture RxR. White would then play PxR, the Pawn becoming a Queen with checkmate. If Black had tried to meet this mating threat by playing RxP (in position 39) White would have mated with R–Kt8, as shown in the above diagram.

39B If, instead of playing RxP, Black had moved his Rook away (say to KB1) White would have played R–Kt8, reaching the above position. Now, if Black cap- tures RxR, White recaptures PxR, the Pawn becoming a Queen with checkmate. If Black makes any other move (instead of RxR) White plays RxRch and then queens the Pawn, winning easily.

39C If, instead of either of the Rook moves in 39A and 39B, Black had played P–R3 (to defend the mating threat explained under 39A) White would have played R– Kt8ch, reaching the above position. Now, the best Black can do is cap- ture RxR and White recaptures PxR, making a Queen with check. This advantage in material wins.

The PRINCIPLE of MOBILITY

IN CHESS, as in war, one of the most important considerations is the "mobility" of the fighting forces. To understand the meaning of this term, as applied to chess, let us first consider the difference between a Queen and a Pawn.

A Queen is said to be worth nine Pawns. Why? What is the real difference between the two men? A Pawn can check and mate the opponent's King just as effectively as the Queen. Each is capable of capturing an enemy piece. However, the Pawn attacks only two squares, while the Queen attacks at long range in eight directions. Even if the entire board is cleared, the Pawn moves only one square at a time, whereas the Queen can cover any distance in one move. In other words, the Queen has much greater *mobility* than the Pawn. This superior mobility gives the Queen great offensive power, makes it much more valuable than the Pawn.

On an open board, the difference between the Queen and Pawn is obvious. But when a game of chess is in progress, the board is *cluttered up with chessmen*. If no men have been exchanged, 32 of the 64 squares are occupied. Of necessity, the Queen must be at least partially obstructed by its own men and the opponent's men. *The more the Queen's mobility is restricted, the less powerful it becomes.* Its effective power depends upon its freedom of movement, its mobility under playing conditions. If the Queen is completely obstructed, it may be as weak or weaker than a Pawn.

Similarly, the factor of mobility affects the powers of all the other chessmen. Rooks become powerful when they possess freedom of movement on files and ranks. Bishops exercise their power when they are free to move along diagonals. The power exercised by any piece depends upon its mobility. Even the Knight, which is able to jump over obstructions, is affected. The Knight's mobility can be restricted by enemy control of the squares within its range, or by the occupation of these squares by friendly pieces.

The war of chess is between two armies of equal force and one of the primary objectives of the successful general is to seek mobility for his forces. The battle for mobility begins with the opening move. At the start, both armies are comparatively immobile. The Queens, Rooks, and Bishops are completely blocked by Pawns so that their offensive power is zero. The main object of the opening moves is to quickly mobilize the important pieces. Each player seeks to develop his pieces on squares where they have freedom of action and exercise their power. As quickly as possible, he mobilizes *all* his important pieces because he realizes that the effective power of the entire army is determined by its overall mobility. One or two men, no matter how mobile and powerful they may be, cannot hope to successfully attack the combined, fully mobilized forces of the enemy.

If one player develops his men quickly and effectively so that his pieces are mobile and exercise a large degree of their potential power, while the opponent develops only one or

two pieces, or places his men in such a way that they interfere with each other and obstruct each other's movements,
*the player with superior mobility possesses a definite ad-
vantage which may be sufficient to win the game.*

SUMMARY

To recapitulate what we have learned, there are three
basic principles which govern the choice of all moves and
affect the strategy and tactics of the entire game:

1. *King Safety.* As the fate of the King determines the
outcome of the game, the King's safety must be considered
at all times. An exposed King is a major weakness. Superior
force or mobility are of no value to a player whose King can
be checkmated.

2. *Material.* The most important winning factor is superiority in material. The player who is ahead in material can
use his advantage to attack the King immediately, or to win
more material and checkmate later, or to force exchanges
and win the endgame.

3. *Mobility.* Superior mobility is an important positional
advantage. The player with greater mobility is employing
the power of his pieces more effectively than his opponent
and has more room to maneuver. The positional advantage
of mobility can be used to attack and win material or to
force checkmate.

HOW MOBILITY WINS

WE HAVE explained that superior force should win. Other factors being equal, the player who is ahead in material should win because he possesses an *absolute* advantage in force. In effect, superior mobility is the equivalent of superiority in material. It represents an *effective* advantage in force which may be sufficient to win. By its nature, however, the advantage of mobility may be temporary, whereas material gain is more likely to be permanent. To produce a win, superior mobility must be utilized to checkmate the opponent, or it must be translated into material gain.

In some chess openings, called "gambits," a Pawn (or even a piece) is sacrificed to obtain quick mobilization and to clear the way for an early attack. The player actually gives up material to obtain the advantages of superior mobility. If the opponent wastes too much time in attempting to hold his material gain at the expense of his own development, the gambit player often succeeds in translating his superior mobility into a winning attack.

The principle of mobility also explains the seemingly mysterious manner in which a strong player defeats a weak opponent to whom he has "given odds." Apart from outright blunders, which may equalize the material forces, the strong player uses the principle of mobility to gain the upper hand. He develops his pieces rapidly, places them on squares on which they exercise their full power. Meantime, his opponent gets his men tangled up so that they possess little or no mobility. His Bishops are hemmed in behind his own Pawns. His Knights are pushed around by the strong player's Pawns. His Rooks never enter the game. Hopefully, he brings his Queen out too soon, then loses time moving it around the board as the strong player attacks it with developing moves. Before long, the advantage of material superiority becomes a negligible factor compared with the effective power of superior mobility, complete mobilization. The strong player then concentrates the power of his mobile forces to win material or to attack the King's defenses and finish with checkmate.

RULES AND EXAMPLES

Lack of mobility may be caused by your opponent's efforts to restrict the freedom of your pieces—or it may be *self-inflicted by your own inferior moves.*

Avoid moves which cause your pieces to interfere with each other. Do not place a piece or Pawn on a square where it blocks the path of another piece and makes it difficult to free the latter.

Favor moves which maintain or increase your freedom of movement and which tend to restrict your opponent's mobility.

There is no rule of thumb which will enable you to pick the best move in any position, but if you try to conform with the principle of mobility in your choice of moves, you will automatically play stronger chess. A knowledge of the importance of mobility serves as a valuable aid to the selection of good moves and weeding out bad moves.

The examples given in the diagrams on these pages help to explain how the principle of mobility governs the choice of moves. These diagrams show various answers which Black could make after the opening moves 1 P–K4, P–K4; 2 Kt–KB3. *Each diagram shows a different second move for Black.* Although every move defends the threat of KtxP, four can be rejected as bad moves because they violate the principle of mobility or endanger the safety of the King. Of the two remaining moves, one stands out as the best method of guarding the threatened Pawn.

1 After 1 P–K4, P–K4; 2 Kt–KB3, Black has played his Bishop to Q3 to defend the threatened Pawn. This is an extremely bad move as it violates the principle of mobility. At Q3, the Bishop blocks the Queen–Pawn which, in turn, imprisons the Queen–Bishop. A striking example of a "traffic jam" which can only be disentangled with loss of time.

2 Instead, Black has played his Queen to K2. The Queen is too valuable to be used for purely defensive purposes. Moreover, the Queen should not be developed so early in the opening as time will be lost if it is attacked. However, this move can be rejected on the grounds of mobility alone as the Queen now blocks the King–Bishop, hampers its development.

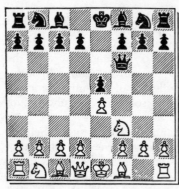

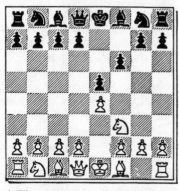

3 Here Black has played his Queen to B3. The Queen's own mobility has been increased but the mobility of the King–Knight has been decreased. The Queen interferes with the KKt, prevents its normal development to KB3. The loss of the Kt's mobility is important, whereas the Queen's added mobility is premature. Avoid moves which cause pieces to interfere with each other.

4 The move 2 ... P–KB3, shown above, is dangerous because it creates a weakness in the King's defenses. White can play 3 KtxP! and if 3 ... PxKt; 4 Q-R5ch, P–Kt3; 5 QxKPch, winning the Rook. Besides, the move does not improve the mobility of Black's important pieces, actually interferes with the development of the King–Knight.

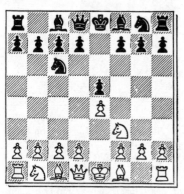

5 The defensive 2 ... P–Q3 is "playable" but the principle of mobility enables us to decide that it is not best. The effect on mobility is double-edged. By moving to Q3, the Q–Pawn has released the Queen–Bishop but has partially shut off the path of the King–Bishop. The move is not bad as it slightly increases over-all mobility.

6 The move 2 ... Kt–QB3 stands out as the best method of guarding the threatened Pawn. Mobilization has been actively promoted by the development of an important piece. The Queen–Knight does not interfere with the mobility of other pieces. There can be no loss of time as the Knight will not be forced to move if threatened by a minor piece.

Illustrative Game

THE GAME portrayed on the following pages is a remarkable example of the effective power of superior mobility. Here you will see the Principle of Mobility in operation. The game was played between Aaron Nimzovich (White) and A. Hakansson in a match at Kristianbad, 1922.

Throughout this entire game, the player of the White forces has one basic idea in mind. His strategy is to *restrict the mobility of his opponent's pieces.* Every move is selected to conform with this fundamental strategy. In the execution of this plan he is successful to a startling degree. The Black pieces are forced to retreat and become completely helpless, forming a tangled cluster of useless wood. Rooks, Bishops and Knights lose all their power as they lose their freedom of movement. Even the mighty Queen is pushed into a corner where she is completely obstructed and utterly useless. Against this jumbled mess of powerless men, the player of the mobile White forces possesses an overwhelming superiority in effective power. His advantage is so great that he is able to sacrifice material to deliver the finishing blow.

The tactics used by the White player are also extremely interesting. You will observe an amazing similarity to the tactics of warfare. Here you will see an example of the "pincers" attack with which all newspaper readers are now familiar. Instead of storming the center of the line, which is usually difficult, White *holds* the center. When the center is blocked, he *attacks on both wings.* Supported by heavier forces in the rear, the Pawn infantry advances on both sides of the board—in a pincers movement which forces the enemy to retreat. When the Pawns have cleared the way, the more powerful forces press home the advantage at the weakest part of the line. A Rook on the QB-file does most of the damage and completes the disorganization of the opposing army. Then comes the final break-through in the center, the storming of the enemy's position to demolish his resistance and win the battle.

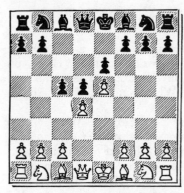

1 The game has started with the moves 1 P–K4, P–K3; 2 P–Q4, P–Q4; 3 P–K5, P–QB4. This is a variation of the "French Defense" which must be played with great care by Black or he will find himself in a permanently cramped position, as in this game.

2 For his 4th move, White has played Q–Kt4. Ordinarily, the early development of the Queen is inadvisable, but this position is exceptional. The Queen cannot be attacked with developing moves by Black and serves a useful purpose at Kt4.

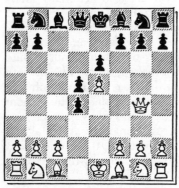

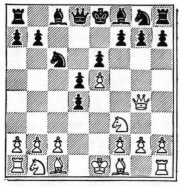

3 The object of White's Queen move is to further hamper the development of Black's King-side pieces. The white KP prevents Black from playing Kt–KB3 and he cannot move his King–Bishop as White would then play QxKtP, attacking and winning the Rook. As shown in the above diagram, Black has played 4...PxP, removing White's support for the KP.

4 White has continued his development with 5 Kt–KB3 and Black has played Kt–QB3. Note that White is delaying the recapture of the Pawn in order to mobilize quickly. He believes he will be able to regain this Pawn at a later stage. Black's Knight is attacking White's KP. He intends to concentrate on this Pawn and try to win it.

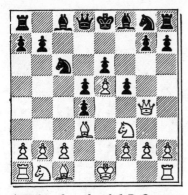

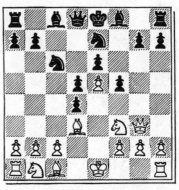

5 White has played 6 B–Q3, continuing his mobilization, and Black has attacked the Queen by playing P–B4. This is not a good move. He hopes that White will play PxP en passant which would enable Black to recapture KtxP, again attacking the Queen with a good developing move and freeing his game. But White does not oblige.

6 Instead, White has played 7 Q–Kt3 and Black has moved his KKt to K2, attempting to solve the problem of how to develop his King-side pieces. Note how the White Queen and Pawn (at K5) are making it difficult for Black to mobilize in a normal manner. His KKt must make another move to free his King–Bishop.

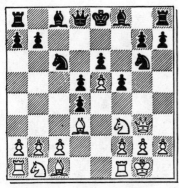

7 For his 8th move, White has castled (8 O–O) and Black has played Kt–Kt3. At last Black seems to have solved the difficulty on his King-side. His KKtP is now shielded from the attack by the White Queen and his KB is free to move. Moreover, both of Black's Kts are now attacking White's KP. So far, this Pawn is safe.

8 White has played 9 P–KR4. Just as Black thought he had solved his problems, he finds that he is in trouble again. White threatens to advance his Pawn to R5, driving the Kt back to K2 where it will again block the Bishop and cramp Black's entire position. Black must now try to answer this threat.

9 Black has answered by playing 9 ... Q–B2. Temporarily, this meets White's threat of P–R5 because Black is now attacking the KP three times and it is defended only twice. If White were to play 10 P–R5, Black could capture the KP with his KKt, winning a Pawn and gaining freedom for all his pieces.

10 But White saw this means of escape and has played 10 R–K1, defending his KP for the third time, so that he again threatens to play P–R5. Black has given up hope of developing his KB and has played B–Q2. His intention is to castle on the Queen's side and possibly work up an attack on the King's wing.

11 White has played 11 P–R3. Does this seem mysterious? After making all the preparations to play P–R5, he suddenly switches over to the other side of the board and moves a Pawn. The explanation is that White has merely postponed playing P–R5. He sees that Black intends to castle QR, so he is preparing a Queen-side attack.

12 Black has castled on the Queen's side (11 ... O–O–O) and White has followed up his last move by playing 12 P–Kt4. Now White's left wing assault is under way. He is executing a pincers attack with his King-side and Queen-side Pawns. Unless Black becomes more aggressive, he will be forced to retreat on both sides.

13 Hemmed in and threatened on both wings, Black should have made a break for freedom by playing P–B5, but he is timid and continues in a defensive role. Fearing the advance of White's QKtP, he has played 12 ... P–QR3. White has continued his nutcracker tactics with 13 P–R5, attacking Black's Kt on the King's side.

14 The Black Kt has retreated to K2, bottling up his undeveloped King–Bishop. Black's mobility, inferior from the start, is disappearing fast. White has played 14 B–Q2. With this move he develops a piece and guards his QKtP so that he can resume the Q-side branch of the pincers attack by advancing his QRP and then his QKtP.

15 Black's forces are becoming crowded into a tangled mass of mutual interference and helplessness. Unable to move a single piece with any effect, he has played 14 ... P–R3 to stop White from playing Kt–Kt5. (Note that White could have played Kt–Kt5 on his last move and raised havoc with Kt–B7, etc., but preferred his own plan of attack.)

16 White has resumed his left-wing advance by playing 15 P–R4, threatening P–Kt5 and the probable disruption of Black's Q-side defenses. Black has countered on the other side with 15 ... P–KKt4. Again he hopes that White will capture PxP en passant as then Black could play R–Kt1 and soon regain his Pawn with attacking chances.

17 But White ignores Black's feeble efforts and has played 16 P–Kt5. Now the Pawn infantry has "contacted the enemy." The advanced White Pawn stabs at the Black Knight and QRP, threatening to capture one or the other and clear the way for the supporting forces in the background. Black has countered with 16 ... P–B5.

18 As White's Queen was attacked, he has played 17 Q–Kt4. Black has retreated his QKt to Kt1 and now this piece is completely stranded, its only function being to guard the attacked RP. Black was afraid to exchange Pawns as this would have opened up the QR-file and exposed his King to attack by White's Rook.

19 Now that Black's QKt is back in its stable, with all the doors locked, White decides not to play PxP which would allow the Kt to come back into the game. Instead, he has played 18 P–B3. Why give away this Pawn when he could have played KtxP? Because White sees a tempting target and is clearing for action.

20 Black has played 18 ... R–K1. He could not afford to take the offered Pawn. White is preparing to attack the Queen and King. Black has no time for material gain when his King is in danger and has moved his Rook to provide an escape square for the Monarch. If he had played 18 ... QPxP, White would have pinned the Pawn with R–QB1.

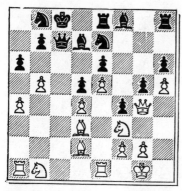

21 White has played 19 PxQP and this capture has opened the QB-file. Now the target is revealed and we see the reason for Black's frantic efforts to get his King out of danger. His Queen and King stand naked and exposed on an open file. White is threatening to play R–QB1 on his next move and then Black's real troubles will begin.

22 Black has hastily moved his King to Q1, to get out of the line of attack, and White has played 20 R–QB1. One of the big guns has moved into position and has opened fire on the disorganized foe. Contrast the power of this Rook, sweeping the entire file with its deadly fire, with the tangled confusion in the enemy camp.

23 Black's attacked Queen has made its one and only playable move—to Kt3. At this point, examine Black's pieces carefully and note how little mobility they possess, how they interfere with each other. Some pieces are completely blocked and cannot move at all; others can make only meaningless, ineffective moves.

24 White has played 21 P–R5 and now the infantry has come to grips with Black's most valuable piece. The QRP stabs at the Black Queen and orders Her Royal Highness to move. But where can she go? Every square but one is commanded by the forces of the White army. The Queen must make an ignominious retreat to escape with her life.

25 The Black Queen has gone back to R2, the only available square, and White has played 22 P–Kt6. Again the Pawn infantry has advanced. Another bayonet thrust, this time by the QKtP, orders the Black Queen to again retreat. Was ever a Queen treated so disrespectfully? The White army is slowly but surely strangling the enemy to death.

26 With only one place to go, the Queen has retreated to R1—and she will sulk in this corner for the rest of the game. Her position is almost incredible. Unable to move, completely hemmed in, it would take a major operation to extricate her. Here is a striking example of how a Queen can lose all her power when she loses her mobility.

27 White decides that the time has come to capitalize on the effective power of his superior mobility. While the pincers attack on the flanks was in progress, the center of the line was blocked, but now White is ready for the final break-through in the center. He has played 23 R–B7—a spearhead thrust into the enemy's vitals.

28 In a struggle to get some freedom, Black has played Kt–B4. This move brings a piece into action and gives some mobility to both his Bishops. His KB can at least move to K2 and his QB may be relieved from guarding the KP. But Black has come to life too late. It would take a long time to disentangle his pieces.

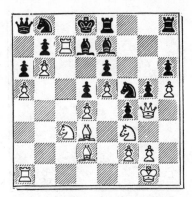

29 White has played 24 Kt–B3.
Hitherto, this Knight has remained dormant, but now White is bringing up his reserves for the final and decisive attack. He intends to demolish the center obstructions. Black has played B–K2, again trying to get his pieces into some semblance of co-ordination and releasing one of his Rooks.

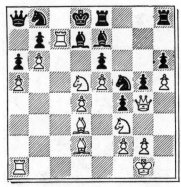

30 Now comes a sparkling finish to the game. White has played 25 KtxQP! The Knight has removed one of the obstructing Pawns in the center and invites capture by the other Pawn to clear the way for the main forces in the rear. If Black plays PxKt, White will play BxKt and the break-through will be effected.

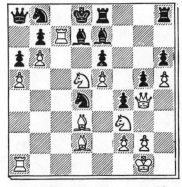

31 Black's defenses are crumbling fast and there is not much he can do to save himself. The center is breaking up and he cannot prevent White from crashing through. He has played KtxP with the idea of regaining the lost Pawn and because he has nothing better. He figures that if White plays KtxKt, he will be able to play PxKt.

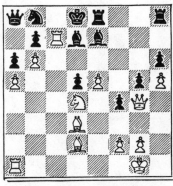

32 The game continues as Black anticipated—up to a point. White has played 26 KtxKt and Black has captured PxKt. Now White's Queen is attacked but Black seems to be unaware of the rude shock that awaits him. Can you see how White will finish this game? He has many ways of winning, but there is a quick and decisive method.

33 White has played 27 QxBch!
The pretty sacrifice of the
Queen is the natural outcome of the
position. White has broken through
the center and is taking advantage
of his overwhelming superiority in
mobility to force a checkmate. The
Black Queen still sulks in the corner,
unable to help her Monarch.

34 Black has played KtxQ, his only
move, and White has delivered
the final blow with 28 Kt–K6 mate!
Even the finish is the result of poor
mobility. The Black King is unable
to move out of check because he is
hemmed in by his own Rook and
Bishop! The entire game is an excellent example of how mobility
wins.

PART THREE

Opening Principles

OUTLINE OF OPENING PRINCIPLES

THE OPENING MOVES of a chess game are extremely important. To play them well you must have the proper objectives in mind. Aimless, purposeless moves lead nowhere and moves made with faulty objectives lead to trouble.

The purpose of the opening is NOT to checkmate your opponent. Abandon all ideas of checkmating in 5 or 6 moves. Any moves which even threaten mate at this stage of the game are probably bad moves unless your opponent has played very weakly. The average game of chess lasts about 40 moves. Checkmate rarely comes before 30 moves have been played. Even the chess champion of the world could not checkmate an ordinary player in much less than 25 moves unless his opponent blundered badly.

Realize, therefore, that if you set out with the idea of checkmating in a few moves, you are breaking the principles of good chess; you are trying to do something which cannot be accomplished against reasonable defense. The moves you make with this false objective in mind are bound to be bad moves which may boomerang and cause your own defeat.

Furthermore, the purpose of the opening is NOT to win material. You may *threaten* to win material but that is not the primary objective of any of your opening moves. You should not particularly expect to win the material you are threatening. Your threats are made for another purpose, as we shall explain later. Of course, you can always take time out to capture a piece if your opponent leaves it "en prise" and if you are sure that you are not falling into a trap—but gaining material in this fashion is the result of a blunder on the part of your opponent.

BASIC OBJECTIVE IS DEVELOPMENT

Major attacks with the definite object of winning material or checkmating the opponent do not normally take place in the opening. The opening is the stage in which the players *prepare* for battle. The basic objective is mobilization, or "development" as it is called in the language of chess.

The chess army is comparatively powerless at the start of the game and the purpose of the opening moves is to *organize and co-ordinate the pieces so that maximum power is made available in the shortest possible time.*

Specifically, this means that *every minor and major piece should be moved from its original square and brought into action as quickly as possible.* The opening moves should be devoted to mobilizing the Knights, Bishops, Queen and Rooks. Development is not completed until the first rank has been cleared of all pieces except the King and Rooks. Furthermore, the King should be castled for his own safety and to bring the castling Rook into play.

This development of the minor and major pieces is the all-important consideration in the opening. In the process, threats are made; but these are opening skirmishes in the battle for mobility, not major engagements to win material. The players fight to control the *central squares* of the board. (This will be fully explained later in this chapter.) Each player seeks maximum mobility for his own forces, attempts to interfere with his opponent's mobilization, tries to make it more difficult for him to develop his pieces in a normal manner.

THE ELEMENT OF TIME

A player who mobilizes *quickly* gains a great advantage over an opponent who wastes time in the opening and fails to develop all his pieces. The preparatory mobilization must be done speedily. If you dawdle in your preparations, the enemy will "git there fustest with the mostest"—and we all know what that means.

The element of time, important in all stages of the game, is particularly decisive in the opening. In chess, "time" is the *number of moves* taken to reach an objective. If two moves are used to do something which could be accomplished in one move, *time* has been wasted.

Opening play is always affected by the opponent's responses, so that the number of moves required to complete development varies with each opening. However, your objective should be the mobilization of ALL your pieces in *as few moves as possible.*

Any useless, unnecessary moves which do not promote the development of your own pieces, or which do not actively interfere with your opponent's development, are a waste of time. Any loss of time in the opening gives your opponent an opportunity to mobilize a more powerful striking force and gain a definite advantage in effective power.

THE IMPORTANCE OF CASTLING

Castling is an essential and integral part of the opening procedure. The King must be transferred to a safe haven and the castling Rook brought into play. As long as your King remains in the center of the board, you are *in danger* and your development is not completed.

Castle at the first opportunity (provided the King will be safe in his castled position, as he should be if you have played the opening properly) and castle on the *King's side* of the board. Don't go in for Queen-side castling until you have gained more experience.

DEVELOPMENT CONDITIONED BY THREATS

Chess is not a game which can be played by rote. Rules and principles are intended as guides to aid the player in selecting good moves and to enable him to follow sound strategical plans.

However, rules should never be followed blindly. For instance, we have emphasized that development is the basic objective of the opening—but this does not mean that you must develop a piece every time you move, no matter what your opponent is doing.

At all times, you must watch your opponent's moves, answer his real threats. Use the principles we have outlined to select your best answer, the reply which develops a piece if possible. But if the threat is important, it must be answered—with or without a developing move.

You must also be on the alert to win material (if it is safe for you to win it), even though this is not your primary objective. Furthermore, there are times when you can postpone your development, to take advantage of certain situations which arise on the board. In other words, the way you play the opening depends to some extent on *how your opponent plays his side of the board.*

WHEN YOUR OPPONENT BREAKS RULES

If your opponent plays in a normal manner and develops his pieces in accordance with the best principles, you should do likewise. Try to interfere with his development; fight to win the battle of mobility—but do NOT break the rules and principles of opening play; do not neglect your own development.

However, if your opponent does not observe opening principles, the situation is changed, and you can adjust your own play accordingly. If he wastes time, *he has given you additional time.* You can then use your own judgment as to the best way of utilizing this advantage. You may decide to continue your development, or you may decide to postpone your development, and use your *extra time* for some other purpose. Moves which would ordinarily be unsound may become the best moves in such positions. If your opponent has played very badly you may see an opportunity to win material or even checkmate him.

If your opponent breaks the rules of opening play by engaging in a premature attack before he has completed his development, it is usually best to concentrate on defense with developing moves. His attack will soon peter out and leave you with a big advantage in development. You can then launch a counter-attack which should be successful. However, if the object of your opponent's "attack" is to win a Pawn and the attack involves considerable *waste of time* on his part, it is usually best to let him have the Pawn. He has given you time to gain an advantage in development which should more than offset the loss of a Pawn. In the opening, the Principle of Mobility is often more important than the Principle of Superior Force.

Your opening play should be flexible and imaginative. Always be ready to take advantage of your opponent's mistakes BUT— and remember this—LET YOUR OPPONENT BE THE FIRST TO NEGLECT HIS DEVELOPMENT AND BREAK THE RULES OF SOUND OPENING PLAY.

MUCH can be learned from a clear understanding of the things one should NOT do. Therefore, let us examine some of the common mistakes made in the opening and demonstrate how and why they lose.

We are not referring now to blunders which cost material or expose you to checkmate. At all stages of the game you must anticipate and answer your opponent's material-winning or mating threats. The mistakes we are now considering are strategical errors. They can be defined in one sentence:

Any opening moves which give your opponent an opportunity to gain an advantage in development are strategical mistakes.

Specifically, mistakes of this nature may be classified as follows:

PREMATURE ATTACKS: Some players are too aggressive for their own good. They start out with the idea of annihilating their opponents in the first ten moves. If an attack is pursued with good developing moves, there can be no criticism of such tactics. Too often, however, these early attacks are made at the expense of development. Premature attacks with two or three pieces are doomed to failure against good defense. The opponent can defend with developing moves and gain an advantage in mobilization which will enable him to counter-attack successfully.

PAWN-GRABBING WITH THE QUEEN: There are other players who are not quite so aggressive, who do not expect to smash the other fellow into smithereens, but who conduct their opening campaign with the idea of stealing one or two Pawns. The Queen is usually used for this purpose and development is postponed while the Pawn-snatching operations are in progress. The loss of time again gives the opponent an advantage in development. Furthermore, Pawn-grabbing is dangerous because the Queen is often trapped and lost.

EXPOSING THE QUEEN TO ATTACK: Early development of the Queen is usually a mistake, whether or not the player intends a premature attack or Pawn-grabbing expedition. If the Queen can be attacked and forced to move a second time, the opponent gains a move and an advantage in development.

UNNECESSARY PAWN MOVES: Beginners often lose time by making needlessly defensive or meaningless Pawn moves. Certain Pawn moves are essential or desirable; others are unnecessary or dangerous.

MOVING THE SAME PIECE TWICE: Sometimes it is necessary or desirable to move the same piece twice in the opening, but if the opponent can thereby gain an advantage in development, the move is a mistake.

On the following pages, the above mistakes are illustrated and explained in more detail.

PREMATURE ATTACKS

AGAINST good defense, a premature attack must fail because it is made *without sufficient preparation*. The attacker tries to break through the enemy defenses with only part of his forces, leaving the remainder undeveloped. As reserves are lacking, the attack dies out. Even if he succeeds in winning material, his unprepared home front is left vulnerable to a strong counter-attack.

It is true that premature attacks sometimes succeed—but only when the defense is weak. It is a mistake to play on the assumption that your opponent will not know how to meet your premature attack. It is much more important that you learn how to play good chess—and a premature attack is not good chess.

Premature attacks are usually made with the Queen and one or two minor pieces. The objective is checkmate or the win of material—both false objectives in the opening. As the Queen is involved, the attacks are extremely risky. In any case, time is wasted—time which should be devoted to mobilization.

Three examples of abortive attempts to win material are given on these pages. In the first game, the English chessmaster Blackburne played the black pieces. The second example is a beginner's effort. If the latter seems crude, note how the same motif, in subtler form, is repeated in the third example, a game played between famous chessmasters Reti and Tartakover.

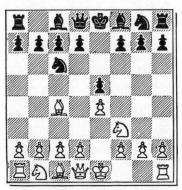

1 This game has opened with the moves 1 P–K4, P–K4; 2 Kt–KB3, Kt–QB3; 3 B–B4. White's third move is one of the strongest at his disposal—better than 3 P–Q4, which we have seen in other games. The Bishop is attacking a vulnerable point in Black's position—his KB2.

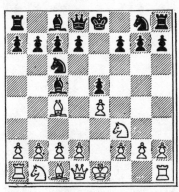

2 Black has replied by playing B–B4, duplicating White's last move. This is one of the oldest openings in chess and is called the Giuoco Piano, meaning "Quiet Game." Actually, this type of opening can lead to lively play. Many traps and pitfalls are involved.

3 White has played 4 BxPch. Without waiting to complete his development he begins an entirely unsound attack. Black has played his defense well and there is no justification for making an attack of this nature. White has sacrificed a piece and to justify this there must be a forced continuation which wins material or checkmates.

4 Black has captured the Bishop with his King and White has played 5 KtxPch. This is the second move in White's unsound "combination." Now he is sacrificing his Knight for a Pawn. Note that Black was not afraid to accept the original Bishop sacrifice. Always accept sacrifices if you see no reason for not doing so.

5 Black has captured KtxKt and White has played 6 Q-R5ch. Now we see the "idea" behind White's attack. He has given up two pieces for two Pawns, but now he must win back one piece. However, this is not sufficient. Black can now play Kt-Kt3, allowing White to capture QxB, and Black will be ahead in material with a winning game.

6 But instead of Kt-Kt3, Black has played P-Kt3 to get out of check. White has continued 7 QxKt. Now the Queen is attacking Black's Bishop and Rook simultaneously. One of these pieces must be lost. Has Black blundered? Has he overlooked this? No, he is deliberately tempting White, leading him on to his destruction.

7 Black has played P–Q3, protecting the attacked Bishop with a Pawn and releasing his other Bishop. White has played 8 QxR. Now count the material and note that White's premature attack has apparently succeeded. He has gained two Pawns and won the exchange (Rook for minor piece). Why did Black allow this? What is his plan?

8 Black has played Q–R5 and now we see why he allowed White to capture his Rook. White's Queen has been deflected from the scene of forthcoming action. His premature attack has left his home front undeveloped and undefended. Black is now launching his counter-attack. He is threatening to play QxBPch, followed by B–Kt5 mate!

9 To defend this threat, White has castled (9 O–O). Black has played Kt–B3, thereby developing a piece and at the same time closing the lid on White's Queen which now cannot retreat to aid in the defense of the home front. Note that Black has a Queen, Bishop and Knight in active play and that his other Bishop is free to jump into action.

10 White has no pieces in action and his King is inadequately defended. He has played 10 P–B3, trying to shut off Black's Bishop with P–Q4, and Black has played Kt–Kt5, threatening QxRP mate. (The Kt move leads to a pleasing finish but Black could have won with 10 ...B–KR6; 11 QxR (if 11 PxB, RxQ), Q–Kt5; 12 P–KKt3, Q–B6 and mate next move.)

11 White has played his only defense to the threatened mate, 11 P–KR3, and Black has forced the issue with BxPch. The White King is in a "mating net," as it is called, and cannot escape. If White now plays RxB, Black will recapture Qx Rch. The White King must then move to R1 (R2 is attacked by the Kt) and Black mates with Q–B8.

12 White has played 12 K–R1, his only move, and Black has played B–KB4, bringing out another piece. Note that this piece can be put "en prise" to a Pawn because the Black Rook now attacks the White Queen. Note also that the Queen cannot escape from the Rook's attack. Every square on the diagonal is attacked by a black piece.

13 White was forced to play 13 QxR or lose his Queen. Black has played QxPch! Black is sacrificing his Queen and demonstrating the helplessness of White's position. White's QR, QKt and QB cannot aid him now because they were never developed. His adventurous Queen is far away—and quite useless.

14 White has played 14 PxQ, his only means of getting out of check, and Black has delivered the final thrust with BxP mate. A delightful, "pure" mate with two Bishops and a Knight. Moral: What is a man profited if he gains a Queen and two Rooks and loses by checkmate? Premature attacks don't pay.

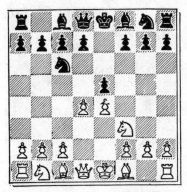

1 In this second example of a premature attack, the game has begun with the opening moves 1 P–K4, P–K4; 2 Kt–KB3, Kt–QB3; 3 P–Q4. We have already seen these starting moves in several games. They are called the "Scotch Opening." White's 3rd move is not the best but it is playable. Better moves are 3 B–B4 or 3 B–Kt5.

2 Black has played PxP and White has recaptured with his Knight (4 KtxP). Then Black developed his Queen prematurely, playing Q–R5. This is a bad move. It is too early to develop the Queen and Black is wasting time trying to win a Pawn with this piece. The motive is wrong and will get him into trouble.

3 For his 5th move, White has returned his Knight to KB3, attacking the Queen, and Black has played QxKPch. This is the type of move which always looks good to a beginner. He captures a Pawn "for nothing" and checks at the same time. The check accomplishes nothing and the Pawn capture is both time-wasting and dangerous.

4 White has played 6 B–K2, getting out of check with a developing move, and Black has played P–Q4. By his Pawn capture, Black has placed his Queen in a dangerous position, exposed to attack. White can gain a big advantage in development by forcing Black to move his Queen again and lose more time.

5 White has castled (7 O–O) and Black has played Kt–Kt5. This horrible move breaks e/ery rule and principle of chess. Black completely disregards the safety of his King and Queen, both dangerously exposed on an open file. He "moves the same piece twice" instead of developing another piece and attempting to safeguard his King.

6 While White is building up a mobile striking force, Black is trying to win material and is paying no attention to his own development or the safety of his King and Queen. White has played 8 R–K1, with an obvious threat, but Black is blind to everything but his own moves and has played KtxBP, moving the Kt for the 3rd time.

7 Black was attacking White's two Rooks with his Knight. Very threatening—but White has calmly captured the Knight with his Queen, playing 9 QxKt. This was no doubt very surprising to the player of the Black pieces who probably said to himself: "The poor fellow doesn't know the game; he is putting his Queen en prise."

8 So Black captured QxQ—and then came the catastrophe! White played 10 B–Kt5 double check! The Bishop checks the King and, in moving, has uncovered a check by the Rook. As the Black King is checked by both pieces, it must move to Q1; whereupon, White will play 11 R–K8 mate and the tale is told.

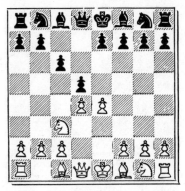

1 This third example of a premature attack, a game played by two chessmasters, bears a remarkable resemblance to the beginner's effort we have just examined. Subtle refinements are added, but the motif is the same. The game has started with the moves 1 P–K4, P–QB3; 2 P–Q4, P–Q4; 3 Kt–QB3. This opening is called the Caro-Kann Defense.

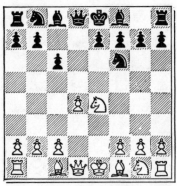

2 Black captured PxP and White recaptured with 4 KtxP. Then Black played Kt–B3, reaching the above position. The object of Black's last move is to develop a piece and at the same time challenge White's Kt which occupies a strong central position. The White Knight is unprotected and Black is threatening to capture it.

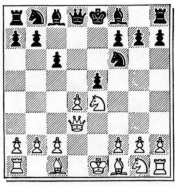

3 To move his Knight away would have been a waste of time and capturing KtxKt would merely aid Black's development (after 5 KtxKt, KPxKt, releasing Black's Bishop). So White has played 5 Q–Q3, defending the Kt, and Black has replied with P–K4. White's Queen move does not violate principles as the Queen is not exposed to attack.

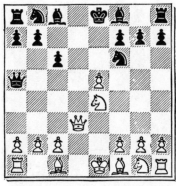

4 Black's last Pawn move was not good as White can capture it and Black must then lose time with his Queen in order to recapture. As shown above, White has played 6 PxP and Black has played Q–R4ch to be able to regain the lost Pawn. If Black had played 6...QxQ White would just recapture PxQ and remain a Pawn ahead.

5 Now White has gained an advantage in development as he played 7 B–Q2 while Black made a second move with his Queen, playing Qx KP. The main reason for Black's Queen maneuver is revealed. He has pinned White's Kt with his Queen and is attacking it twice. Apparently White must defend with P–KB3, but then Black will play B–KB4.

.6 But instead of wasting time with a non-developing Pawn move, which would only temporarily defend the threat, White shows that Black's attack is premature. He has castled (8 O–O–O) and allowed Black to capture KtxKt! Black has won a piece but will lose the game. The refutation of Black's tactics is brilliant and convincing.

7 White has played 9 Q–Q8ch!! By this startling sacrifice of the Queen, White demonstrates that Black has failed to observe the principles of opening play, has wasted time with his Queen and captured material at the expense of development, has thereby exposed himself to a counter-attack which ends the game with amazing rapidity.

8 Black has played KxQ and White has given a deadly double check by playing 10 B–Kt5. The finish is similar to the last example, with this added refinement: if Black now plays K–K1, then 11 R–Q8 is mate, or if he plays K–B2, 11 B–Q8 is mate. Moral: Premature attacks may win material but often lose the game.

PAWN-GRABBING WITH THE QUEEN

SOME PREMATURE ATTACKERS go out for big game. They threaten mate, try to win a piece, or the exchange. They throw everything they have at their opponent, including the proverbial kitchen sink. Some of these attacks are hard to meet and call for skillful defense. Against weak players they often succeed. The attacks may be theoretically unsound but the defense must be accurate.

There is, however, another type of premature attacker who has no such lofty ambitions. He is the player who brings out his Queen as quickly as possible, hoping to win one or two Pawns with this powerful piece and then return to safety. The Pawn-grabber does not expect to checkmate you, or win important material; he is just after a Pawn or two.

This type of premature attack is particularly reprehensible. The booty is so small—and the risk is so great. The Queen, like a large and powerful battleship without a convoy, is in constant danger if she is exposed to attack before the minor pieces have been developed. The Queen is far too valuable a piece to be risked in this fashion. Not only is time lost—the Queen herself may be lost.

The following two examples illustrate the dangers of Pawn-grabbing with the Queen.

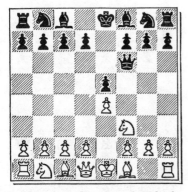

1 This game has opened with the moves 1 P–K4, P–K4; 2 Kt–KB3, Q–B3. Black's Queen move is premature and interferes with the development of the KKt. His objective is wrong. Good players develop their minor pieces first, then castle, then bring the Queen into play.

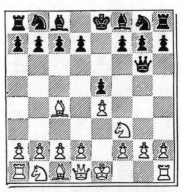

2 White has played 3 B–B4, developing another piece, and Black has played Q–KKt3. Now we see that he brought out the Queen to win a Pawn. He is attacking the White KP and KKtP. But he is wasting time and rapidly losing the opening battle of mobility.

3 White has played 4 P–Q3, protecting his KP and releasing his
Queen–Bishop which now becomes
an active piece on the diagonal even
though it has not yet been moved.
Black has played QxP, grabbing a
loose Pawn with his Queen. Black
has now moved his Queen three
times, neglecting his development
to win a Pawn.

4 White is already far ahead in
mobilization and Black's Queen
is in a dangerously exposed position.
White has played 5 R–Kt1, attacking the Queen, and Black has played
Q–R6—the only square of escape.
With each move, White has
brought a different piece into play
while Black has just moved his
Queen around.

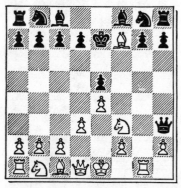

5 White now capitalizes on his big
advantage in development and
exploits the exposed position of the
Black Queen. He has played 6 BxPch
and Black has moved his King to
K2. Black could not capture KxB as
then White would have played Kt–
Kt5ch, attacking both King and
Queen and winning the Queen.

6 However, the errant Queen is lost
in another way. White has played
7 R–Kt3 and Her Majesty is cor-
nered. The Rook threatens her life
and there is no way to escape. Every
square to which the Queen can
move is attacked by the White
forces. Black won his Pawn but paid
a high price for it.

154

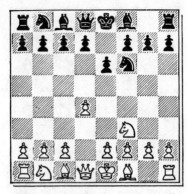

1 Here is another example of the dangers involved in Pawn-grabbing with the Queen. The game has opened with 1 P–Q4, Kt–KB3; 2 Kt–KB3, P–K3. This is one of the many variations of the Queen's Pawn Opening. The original Pawn advance is just as good a starting move as 1 P–K4 and is preferred by many chessmasters.

2 White has continued with 3 B–Kt5 and Black has played P–B4, attacking White's Pawn in the center. White's move developed a minor piece and the Bishop now pins the Black Knight. The Knight cannot move without exposing the Queen to capture. Black's reply threatens White's Pawn and tempts him to capture.

3 It would not be good for White to play PxP as this would merely aid Black's development; Black could recapture BxP and his Bishop would be mobilized. Instead, White has played 4 P–K4 and threatens to advance this Pawn to K5, attacking the pinned Knight. Black must do something about this threat.

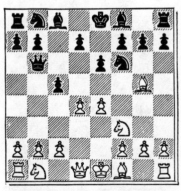

4 Black has played 4...Q–Kt3. This answers White's threat. If White now plays P–K5, the Kt can move as it is no longer pinned. Moreover, this Kt now attacks White's unguarded KP. White must move or guard this Pawn—or capture the Knight. Black's Queen is also threatening to capture White's QKtP and win the Rook.

155

5 White must reply to Black's counter-attack with care. To play BxKt would be an easy solution but instead he gives his opponent an opportunity to blunder. He has played 5 QKt–Q2, guarding the KP and inviting Black to play QxP. Note, however, that 5 Kt–B3 would not do as Black could then play QxP with impunity.

6 Black has played 5...QxP. If White's QKt had been played to B3, this capture would be safe as the Queen would be attacking the Kt. Now it is a waste of time and dangerous. White has continued 6 Kt–B4 attacking the Queen. Where can the Queen go? There are only 3 squares not attacked. Only one seems safe.

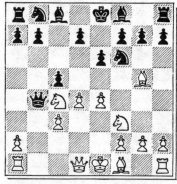

7 Black played 6...Q–Kt5ch and White replied with 7 P–B3 forcing the Queen to move again. Note that if Black had played 6...Q–B6ch, White would have answered 7 B–Q2 and the Queen would have been lost. Or if he had played 6... Q–Kt4, White would have played 7 Kt–Q6ch, followed by 8 BxQ.

8 In position 7, Black's Queen had only two possible moves: QxPch or Q–Kt4. The latter would have been answered as explained under diagram 7. So Black has played 7 ...QxPch and White has trapped the Queen by playing 8 B–Q2. Again Black won a Pawn but paid for it with his Queen.

EXPOSING THE QUEEN TO ATTACK

IT IS CHARACTERISTIC of premature attacks that the powerful Queen is brought out as soon as possible to give the attack force. It should be noted that this early development of the Queen is generally *a mistake in itself.* Even if a player has no intention of conducting a premature attack, he should not place his Queen in an exposed position in the early stages of development. If the Queen can be attacked and forced to move a second time, a move has been wasted and the opponent gains an advantage in development.

The diagrams below illustrate this point. Here the opening moves of the "Center Game" are pictured.

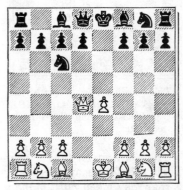

1 The opening begins with the moves 1 P–K4, P–K4; 2 P–Q4. White's second Pawn move is premature.

2 Black captured PxP and White recaptured with his Queen. Then Black played Kt–QB3, reaching this position.

White may have had no intention of conducting a premature attack. However, by playing 2 P–Q4 and then recapturing the Black Pawn with his Queen, *he exposed his Queen to attack.* Black's developing response of 3 ... Kt–QB3, shown in position No. 2, forces White to move his Queen a second time. He usually moves it to K3—but this is a wasted move. Black can immediately gain an advantage in development by bringing out his other Knight. Thus, in four opening moves, Black develops two Knights while White develops nothing but his Queen. We need pursue the opening no farther to conclude that it is inferior for White.

Another example of losing time with the Queen is found in the opening illustrated below.

Black's defense can be rejected as definitely inferior because it entails loss of time when his Queen is attacked. White obtains a big lead in development. (In position No. 2 Black usually plays 4 ... Q–K3 and the continuation is 5 B–Kt5ch, B–Q2; 6 O–O.)

1 This opening begins with the moves 1 P–K4, P–K4; 2 Kt–KB3, P–Q4. Black's second Pawn move is premature.

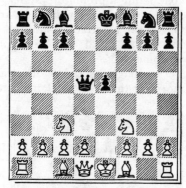

2 White played 3 PxP and Black recaptured with his Queen. Then White played 4 Kt–B3, reaching this position.

There are many similar examples to be found in the openings. They should be avoided on principle. The point to remember is that the Queen *must move* if it is attacked by a minor piece or Pawn which cannot be captured. As a result, the opponent gains a move and a corresponding advantage in development.

It should be borne in mind, however, that there are a few occasions when the early development of the Queen is a strong move. Such moves are distinguished by the fact that *no loss of time is involved*. The opponent does not gain an advantage in development.

UNNECESSARY PAWN MOVES

THE TYPE of player who goes in for premature attacks at least possesses the fighting spirit and will to win which characterizes all good chessplayers. His efforts are ill-timed as the attacks are made without sufficient preparation; but experience will correct this fault.

On the other hand, many inexperienced players approach the game with far too defensive a point of view. Psychologically, this type of player is beaten before he makes his first move. He is scared of his opponent and would never dream of making a premature attack—or any other kind of attack. He is forever "seeing spooks" and warding off fancied threats before they materialize.

The defensive player loses time and fails to accomplish the purpose of the opening by making *unnecessary moves* to protect himself from imagined danger. Moves of this type are also made by players who may not be consciously on the defensive, but who just don't know what to do. Unaware of the true purpose of the opening, they make meaningless moves which accomplish nothing.

A chess move should never be made without reason. It must have a purpose behind it. Even if the objective is wrong, this is better than no objective at all. If you keep in mind the fact that you are supposed to develop your pieces in the opening, you will automatically avoid the useless and needlessly defensive moves made by most beginners; you will learn to make every move count.

Most of the unnecessary opening moves made by weak players are Pawn moves. A favorite is Pawn to KR3 or Pawn to QR3, played when the Pawn attacks nothing and defends no real threat. The move in itself is not bad; it is the timing which makes it a mistake. Strong players often play P–R3, but only when it is a useful, necessary move. If the Pawn attacks a Bishop or Knight it may be a perfectly good move; no time is lost, since the opponent is forced to move a developed piece. Occasionally, the move is necessary to defend an important threat. But to play P–R3 before your pieces are developed and without any real reason for the move is just a futile waste of time.

Another common but frequently unnecessary move is Pawn to Q3 when a piece move would accomplish the same purpose and when the position calls for P–Q4 at a later stage. Equally time-consuming but much more dangerous are unnecessary moves of the Pawns guarding the castled King. In openings which begin with the move 1 P–K4 (King-Pawn Openings) it is particularly dangerous for Black to move his King-Bishop Pawn. Any Pawn move which will make it difficult for the player to castle or which will render the King unsafe in his castled position is a bad move.

Actually, most openings require *only a few Pawn moves*. It is, of course, essential that certain Pawns be moved in order that the Bishops and Queen may be developed. Pawns are also played to occupy and control the important central squares of the board, or to contest the opponent's occupation of these squares. In practically all openings, the *King-Pawn and Queen-Pawn are played at an early stage* because the movement of these Pawns achieves both the above objectives. Pieces are released for action and at the same time the Pawns occupy central squares. In some openings, the King and Queen Pawns are the only Pawns moved during the early stages of development.

In the popular "Queen's Gambit" and in a few other openings, the Queen-Bishop Pawn is moved in addition to the QP and KP. Other Pawns are played in special openings. In all cases, however, a strong player moves a Pawn only when a definite and important reason exists for the move. The Pawn is played to permit the development of a piece, or to occupy an important square, or to attack an enemy piece, or to restrict the opponent's mobility. He avoids all Pawn advances which will endanger the safety of his King. He very seldom moves a Pawn for purely defensive reasons; if possible, he defends a threat by developing a piece and thereby avoids loss of time.

The initial Pawn moves of standard openings are easily learned. The wisdom of these moves has been established. After making these Pawn advances, the learner should question any subsequent Pawn move which he contemplates making. Is it really necessary to move the Pawn? Is it not possible to develop a piece instead?

And how about piece moves? All the unnecessary moves are not made with Pawns. If you make two moves with the same piece, when it could be developed with one move, you are probably making an unnecessary move and losing time. Shifting the same piece around the board does not develop your other pieces. Moreover, if you violate the Principle of Mobility you may be forced to make unnecessary moves to untangle pieces which interfere with each other.

The loss of time caused by unnecessary moves is a serious matter in the opening. Each wasted move is a net gain for the opponent. If you present him with one extra move the gain is slight; perhaps you are strong enough to survive this handicap. But if you waste two or three moves you will find yourself in hot water. Any worthy opponent can use two or three extra moves to develop a strong position and make you suffer for your sins.

By way of entertainment and instruction, let us examine three examples of faulty opening play in which unnecessary, time-wasting moves are made. The first gamelet illustrates the strong position which can be built up in a few moves against a player who makes defensive Pawn moves instead of developing his pieces. The second example is a game played by Alexander Alekhine, chess champion of the world, against an amateur in a simultaneous exhibition. Unnecessary moves and failure to provide for the King's safety result in a quick finish. The third example is a game played between two High School boys in the 1943 tournament for the Interscholastic Championship of New York. In this game, the player of the white pieces is afraid of his own shadow, breaks all the opening rules, defeats himself with meaningless moves.

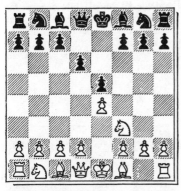

1 The opening moves: 1 P–K4, P–K4; 2 Kt–KB3, P–Q3. Black's 2nd move was inferior but not exactly a wasted move as the Q–Bishop was released. However, White's threat could have been answered by developing a piece. Either the defensive Kt–QB3 or the counter-attacking Kt–KB3 is a better move than P–Q3.

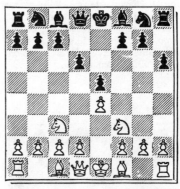

2 White's 3rd move was Kt–B3 and Black played P–KR3. Black's Pawn move was completely unnecessary. It attacks nothing, defends nothing, does not promote development in any way. In three moves, White has developed two pieces while Black has made three Pawn moves and developed no pieces at all.

161

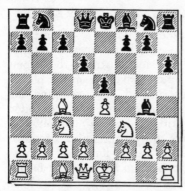

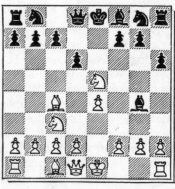

3 White's 4th move was B–B4 bringing out another piece, and at last Black has moved a piece by playing B–Kt5. Note that after the initial Pawn move, White has brought a different piece into action with each successive move. Meantime, Black has frittered away valuable time with unnecessary, nondeveloping Pawn moves.

4 Much to Black's surprise, no doubt, White has played 5 KtxP!! The Knight which Black thought he had pinned with his Bishop has captured the KP and White exposes his Queen to capture! White is so far ahead in development that he can give up his Queen to carry out his plan, which is nothing less than checkmate!

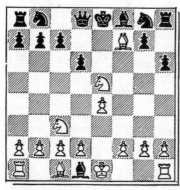

5 Black failed to foresee the consequences of accepting the sacrifice and captured BxQ. Whereupon, White continued with 6 Bx-Pch! Black should not have taken the Queen. In position 4, he should have captured PxKt, when White would have played QxB with a Pawn ahead, which would be enough to win but would take longer.

6 Black has played K–K2, his only move to get out of check, and White delivered the knockout blow with 7 Kt–Q5 mate! This shows what can happen when one player mobilizes while the other wastes time. Even if Black had not taken the Queen, White's gain of a Pawn and advanced development would have won the game.

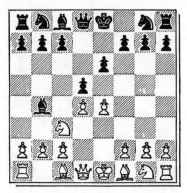

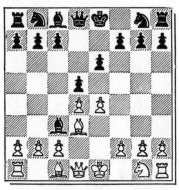

1 As pictured above, this second example has begun with the moves 1 P–K4, P–K3; 2 P–Q4, P–Q4; 3 Kt–QB3, B–Kt5. This is a variation of the French Defense. Black is now threatening to play PxP and White cannot recapture with his pinned Kt. White must find an answer to this threat on his next turn.

2 White has defended the Pawn by playing 4 B–Q3 and Black has captured BxKtch. Black's capture is not good. It is seldom a good idea to exchange a developed piece, which is serving a useful purpose, unless forced to do so. Black's Bishop was pinning the Knight and there was no reason for releasing the pin.

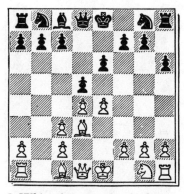

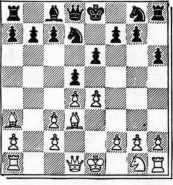

3 White has completed the exchange of minor pieces by playing 5 PxB and Black has played P–KR3. Again we see this inexplicable, time-wasting Pawn move. Without a single piece in action, Black makes a useless move and presents his opponent (world's champion!) with the equivalent of an extra turn.

4 White has gratefully accepted the favor and has developed an-other piece by playing 6 B–R3. This Bishop now rakes the Black King's position and makes it difficult for Black to castle. Instead of trying to solve this problem, Black has played Kt–Q2, bottling up his Q–Bishop with an irrelevant move. He should have played Kt–K2.

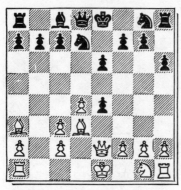

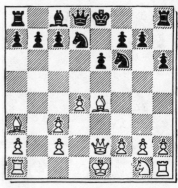

5 White has continued with 7 Q–K2 and Black has replied by capturing PxP. Black's capture is understandable. White was threatening to win a Pawn with 8 PxP as Black's pinned KP could not recapture. But Black could have defended this threat by playing Kt–K2 which develops another piece and permits castling later.

6 White has completed the exchange of Pawns with 8 BxP and Black has played KKt–B3. With this move Black has made castling impossible. Behind in development, he cannot afford to leave his King in an exposed position. His urgent problem was to find a means of castling. Again he could have accomplished this by playing Kt–K2.

7 White has retreated his attacked Bishop, playing 9 B–Q3. On the brink of disaster, Black has innocently and unsuspectingly played another Pawn move—P–QKt3. He is trying to develop his Bishop; but he has already lost too much time. His only chance of survival was to play Kt–Kt3 but he would not have lasted long.

8 White has played 10 QxPch and the game is over! If Black plays PxQ, White checkmates with B–Kt6! Or if Black interposes his Queen, then QxQ is mate. Spectacular finishes like this are always possible against a player who wastes time with unnecessary moves and fails to provide for the safety of his King.

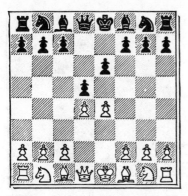

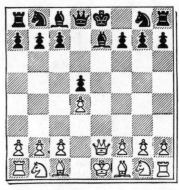

1 This third example started with the moves 1 P–K4, P–K3; 2 P–Q4, P–Q4. These are the opening moves of the French Defense. Note that in the King–Pawn Openings, if Black plays a defense which permits White to play P–Q4 without losing a Pawn, White makes this move immediately. This is a good rule to remember.

2 The game has continued with the moves 3 PxP, PxP; 4 Q–K2ch, B–K2, reaching the above position. White's check is a typical beginner's move. It is too early to decide where to develop the Queen and the check does Black no harm. Hence, it is a wasted move. Worse still, White's Queen now blocks his own K–Bishop.

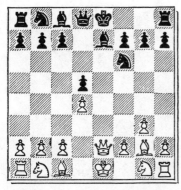

3 This position was reached after 5 P–KKt3, Kt–KB3; 6 B–Kt2 White has wasted another move as it has taken two moves to develop his Bishop. Meantime, his Queen and King are dangerously exposed on an open file. White's chief concern now should be to provide for castling as soon as possible and safeguard his King.

4 Black played 6...B–Kt5, attacking the Queen, and White replied with 7 P–KB3?? Wasted move No. 3 and a perfect example of how not to play chess. It was unnecessary as Kt–KB3, developing a piece and providing for castling, serves the purpose. The Pawn move demobilizes the KB and KKt, endangers the King.

5 Black played 7...B–B4 and White again attacked the Bishop with 8 P–KKt4. Another pointless, unnecessary and weakening move. White's only hope of quick castling is on the King-side. The Pawn advance makes this hazardous. In any case, the attack itself is meaningless as Black can just move his Bishop.

6 Black retreated his Bishop to Q2 and White, believe it or not, played 9 P–QR3??? With his King and Queen in danger and not a single piece in play, except the Queen, he makes another time-wasting Pawn move! He is activated by fear of a non-existent threat. At least he should have played Kt–KR3 to permit castling.

7 Black castled and then followed 10 B–K3, B–Q3; 11 Kt–R3, reaching this position. With a sudden spurt of energy, White has actually developed two pieces in two moves! But he has come to life too late. By this time he should have been fully developed and his King in a safe position. As it is, he is in great danger.

8 The game has continued with 11 ...R–K1; 12 Kt–B3, P–B4; 13 Q–Q3, reaching this position. White failed to realize the urgency of castling. He should have taken the King out of danger on his 12th move instead of playing Kt–B3. He would probably have lost the game anyhow, but it would have taken longer.

166

9 As it is, White's goose is cooked.
   In position 8, Black was threatening PxP and general havoc in the White camp as the pinned Bishop could not recapture. White moved his Queen in an attempt to meet this threat. But, as shown above, after 13 ... PxP; 14 QxP, Kt–B3, White is still in trouble.

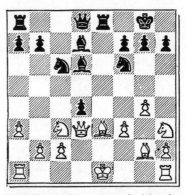

10 White's Queen, attacked by the Kt, has retreated to Q3 and Black has played P–Q5! Another Black Pawn renews the same threat as before. The pinned Bishop is as defenseless as a sitting duck. White is beginning to pay the penalty for his time-wasting moves and failure to castle when he had the opportunity to do so.

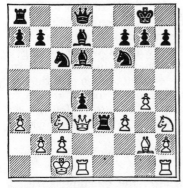

11 In desperation White has castled on the Queen-side (16 O–O–O) and Black has played RxB, attacking the Queen. There was no way for White to avoid losing the piece and now he is falling apart at the hinges. He must move his Queen and then he will lose his Knight as well. White could resign here but didn't.

12 White retreated his Queen to Q2 and Black played RxKt! At this point White should resign as he has lost two pieces and if he plays PxR he will be mated. The finishing moves, from the position in the above diagram, are as follows: 18 PxR, BxPch; 19 K–Kt1, Q–Kt3ch; 20 K–R1, Q–Kt7 mate.

167

MOVING THE SAME PIECE TWICE

THE LOSS OF TIME caused by irrelevant, unnecessary Pawn moves is fairly obvious. There are, however, other ways of wasting time in the opening which are not always apparent to the player.

Let us consider the opening moves pictured in the diagrams below:

 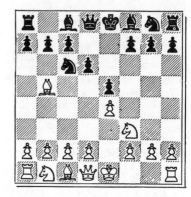

The first diagram shows the position after 1 P–K4, P–K4; 2 Kt–KB3, Kt–QB3; 3 B–K2. The second diagram shows the position after the succeeding moves of 3 ... P–Q3; 4 B–Kt5. After Black moved his QP, White decided it would be a good idea to pin the Knight. But he could have played his Bishop to Kt5 in the first place and saved a move. He used two moves to accomplish something which could have been done in one move.

This is a rather crude example of what is called "losing a tempo." A move is wasted and the opponent gains an extra turn. Here the two Bishop moves were made in succession and the loss of time is apparent. However, players often lose a tempo in exactly this fashion, without realizing it, because a few moves may intervene between the two moves of the Bishop, or whichever piece is moved twice.

In the diagrams on the next page, another method of losing a tempo is illustrated.

At the left is shown the position after the opening moves, 1 P–K4, P–K3; 2 B–B4. At the right appears the position after Black's response of 2 ... P–Q4. Now, whether or not White exchanges Pawns, he must move his Bishop a second time *without accomplishing anything* with this piece. If he checks with the Bishop (at Kt5) he will lose even more time when Black responds with P–B3. Obviously, White should not have played 2 B–B4. By this faulty development of his Bishop, he is forced to make a useless move with this piece in response to his opponent's strong and logical 2 . . . P–Q4. In effect White has lost a valuable tempo.

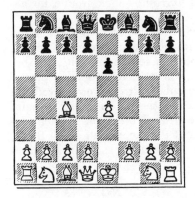 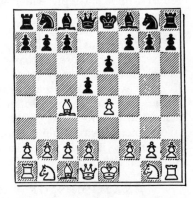

These two examples are purposely of an elementary nature to clearly illustrate the meaning of a loss of tempo. In the first case, the loss of a move is clearcut and absolute. In the second case, the effect is the same; the Bishop is forced to make an additional, useless move and the opponent gains the advantage of a tempo.

Needless to say, time-wasting moves of this type are not always as obvious as this. Moreover, it does not follow that a tempo is lost every time a piece is moved twice in the opening. As always, the opponent's play affects each situation on the board. It is only when the opponent *gains time to make a strong move* that a loss is sustained by the player who moves a piece twice.

The lesson to be learned is that unnecessary moves are always a waste of time, whether they are made voluntarily or are forced upon you. A piece should be developed with ONE MOVE—not two moves, or three moves. Furthermore, each piece should be developed on a square where it is free from harmful attack, where it cannot be forced away by a strong reply.

To apply this lesson, you must learn to distinguish between good and bad developing moves. As we shall explain later, a good developing move usually threatens something, or attacks a weak point in the enemy's position, or interferes with the opponent's development. The force of the move is nearly always directed towards the center of the board, the area of greatest mobility.

You must also learn *never to make a move without considering your opponent's possible replies.* In fact, this is one of the best ways of judging whether your contemplated move is good or bad. If your move will *hurt your opponent* and force him to make an inferior move in reply, then you have found an excellent move. Even if he is forced to make a defensive or mediocre response there is probably nothing wrong with your own move. But if you see that he has a reply which will *hurt you*—look around for another move!

As you gain experience, you will learn *how to time* your developing moves. In the captions to the various examples in this course, you will observe that a move is sometimes criticized because "it was too early to decide where to develop this piece." In other words, there was no particularly strong move available to the piece in question. In such cases the player should usually delay the development of the piece until the right moment arrives, when it is possible to bring out the piece with a real threat and employ its full force. In the meantime, some other piece should be developed.

EXAMPLES OF TIME-WASTING PLAY

On the following pages we give three brief examples of faulty opening play in which the above rules are broken. In the first example, Black tries to lay a trap for his opponent but in doing so he makes a useless second move with a developed piece; the piece is driven away and Black loses two tempi. In the second example Black does not time his moves properly and fails to consider the replies available to his opponent; as a result, he is forced to retract his only developing moves. The third is a similar case, but here the player gets into still more trouble by refusing to admit his error.

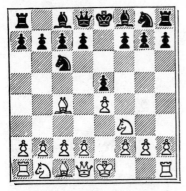

1 In this example the game has opened 1 P–K4, P–K4; 2 Kt–KB3, Kt–QB3; 3 B–B4. These are standard moves we have seen in other games. Black should now play either 3 ... B–B4 or 3 ... Kt–B3, in either case observing opening principles by developing a piece on a strong square.

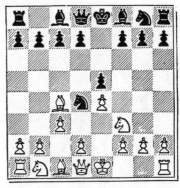

2 Instead, Black has broken the rules by playing Kt–Q5 and White has attacked the Kt with 4 P–B3. Black has not only wasted a move which should have been used to develop another piece, but has placed the Kt on a square where it can be driven away and forced to make another useless move.

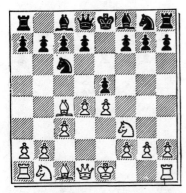

3A Black has returned his Kt to B3 and White has played 5 P–Q4. As a result of Black's two useless moves with his Kt, White has gained two tempi. Compare this position with diagram 1. In each case it is Black's turn to play. Black's position is unchanged but White has made two Pawn moves. He has been presented with two extra moves.

3B From the position of diagram 2, Black has played KtxKt (instead of Kt–QB3) and White has played 5 QxKt. Again White has gained two tempi. Black's Kt made 3 moves to capture a piece which had made only one move. (The trap: Black hoped for 4 KtxP?, Q–Kt4; 5 KtxBP, QxKtP; 6 R–B1; QxKPch; 7 B–K2, Kt–B6 mate.)

171

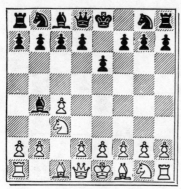

1 This second example has started
with 1 P–QB4, P–K3; 2 Kt–
QB3, B–Kt5. White's 1st move is
called the English Opening, infre-
quently used. Black's 2nd move with
his Bishop was premature. It is too
early to determine the best square
for this piece. 2 ... P–Q4 was more
logical.

2 White has continued with 3 P–
K4 and Black has played Kt–KB3.
If Black had first considered his
opponent's replies he would not have
made this Kt move. He has placed
his Kt on a square where it can be
attacked and driven away with loss
of time. 3 ... Kt–K2 would have
been playable.

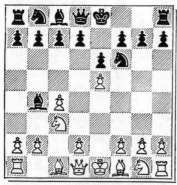

3 White has played 4 P–K5 and
this will force Black to return his
Kt to Kt1, thereby losing two moves.
If Black tries to justify his move by
now playing BxKt, followed by Kt–
K5, he will lose the game. (4 ...
BxKt, 5 QPxB, Kt–K5?; 6 Q–Kt4,
Kt–B4; 7 QxKtP, R–B1; 8 B–Kt5,
P–KB3; 9 BxP, RxB; 10 PxR, etc.)

4 Black played 4 ... Kt–Kt1, returning his Kt to its original
square and then followed 5 Q–Kt4,
B–B1. Black has retracted both his
piece moves and White has gained
4 tempi! Black's retreat of his Bishop
was the best way to defend White's
threat of QxKtP, winning a Rook.
Faulty timing caused this debacle.

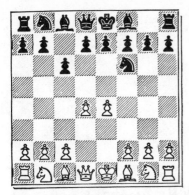

1 In this third example we again
see the effect of faulty timing of
opening moves and failure to anticipate the opponent's replies. The
game has started with 1 P–K4, P–
QB3; 2 P–Q4—the Caro-Kann Defense. At this point Black should
play 2 . . . P–Q4, the logical follow-
up of his first move.

2 Instead, he first played 2 . . .
Kt–B3 and after White's response
of 3 B–Q3 he then played 3 . . . P–
Q4. This transposition of moves was
a bad mistake as White then continued with 4 P–K5, as shown here.
Black should have considered this
possibility before making his second
move.

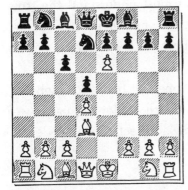

3 Unwilling to admit that he made
a mistake (he should have returned his Kt to Kt1) Black has
played KKt to Q2 and White has
continued with 5 P–K6! Black cannot take the Pawn or he will be
mated. (5 . . . PxP; 6 Q–R5ch, P–
Kt3; 7 QxPch, PxQ; 8 BxP mate.)

4 So Black moved his attacked Kt
back to B3 and White captured
6 PxPch! Now Black must play KxP
and lose the privilege of castling. By
faulty timing, not considering his
opponent's replies and unwillingness
to admit his error, Black has lost
much time and will lose more.

173

CORRECT OPENING STRATEGY

WE HAVE demonstrated that premature attacks, pawn-grabbing, time-wasting moves and other strategical mistakes in the opening lead to a lost game. We have learned that the opening should be devoted to mobilization—the development of all the pieces. But how should the pieces be developed? On what squares should they be placed—and why should they go there?

To answer these questions you must understand the true strategy of the opening. When you comprehend this fundamental strategy you will know how to develop your pieces on the most effective squares.

The real strategical aim of the opening battle for mobility is *control of the central squares*. On the following pages we explain what this means and how it affects opening development.

CONTROL OF THE CENTER

THE CENTRAL SQUARES, outlined with a heavy rule in the diagram below, are the four squares in the exact center of the board—K4, Q4, K5 and Q5. These are the all-important squares around which the opening battle rages. The squares surrounding this area, outlined with a broken line in the diagram, are next in importance, as these are subsidiary to the center.

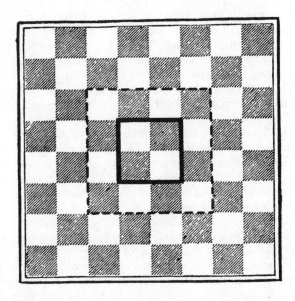

The entire central area is important because this is the region of the board in which pieces exercise their maximum offensive and defensive power and in which they possess their greatest mobility. The player who is able to *use* central squares has great freedom of action and is able to transfer his pieces quickly from one side of the board to the other. If his pieces are located in or near the center, they attack more squares—and more important squares—than elsewhere on the board. This is particularly true of Knights. A Knight posted at K5 or Q5, which cannot be captured or driven away, is a tower of strength and much more powerful than a Knight located at the side of the board. In the center, the Knight attacks 8 important squares; at the edge of the board, say at R3, it attacks only 4 squares and the squares are less important. The Queen and Bishops are also powerful when they are in or near the center of the board In the early stages of the game these pieces do not ordinarily *occupy* squares in the exact center, but their power is directed *towards* the center. Bishops are frequently placed on squares subsidiary to the center (KB4, QB4, K3 or Q3). Rooks are also used to support the center, not to occupy it.

It is logical that the center of the board should be the field of battle in the opening, for you can hit at the center from all directions—from the left and right with your Knights and Bishops, straight ahead with your Pawns and Rooks, from any angle with the Queen. In other words, it is possible to concentrate your fire on the center with great rapidity. By the same token, of course, your opponent can defend the center with equal facility. In chess, as in war, it is not easy to break through in the center of the line. The player of the white pieces, who has the opening initiative, does not really expect to crash through in the center and win the game in this manner. Nevertheless, he begins by concentrating the power of his forces on the central squares in the hope of establishing even a minute advantage in this sector because he knows that this advantage will enable him to exert continuous pressure on his opponent, slightly cramp his mobility, make it easier to execute wing attacks at a later stage in the game. If, in the process, Black wavers in his defense and allows White to establish a clear superiority in the center, the game may be won on this factor alone.

If a player loses control of the center he is in the position of a General whose army is divided by a wedge in the center of his line. He lacks mobility and means of communication. Unable to occupy squares in or near the center, his pieces are badly placed. If the center wedge is strong enough, it may completely disrupt his position. An early break-through in the center (unusual against good defense) can win with alarming speed.

As White has the opening move, he has the best chance of securing an advantage in the center. With each succeeding move he attacks the center, directly or indirectly, and endeavors to obtain control of at least one of these vital squares. (To *control* a central square means that you have established the right to place one of your pieces on this square without having it captured. You may or may not exercise your right of occupancy— but the square is yours. It also means that you can capture an enemy piece if it is placed on the square you control.)

Black fights back and tries to prevent White from establishing control in the center. If given the opportunity, of course, Black will wrest the initiative from White and secure an advantage in the center for himself. Against a worthy opponent, however, Black is satisfied if he is able to establish *equality* in the center. He may accomplish this by liquidating the center Pawns or he may be able to offset White's control of one square by commanding the corresponding square in White's camp.

PAWNS IN THE CENTER

Pawns perform an extremely important function in the control and occupation of central squares. When a Pawn occupies a central square it attacks two vital squares in the enemy's territory and prevents him from placing pieces on these squares. If there is no opposing Pawn to dispute the attack on one of these squares, the Pawn then *controls* this square and its value is greatly enhanced. This is illustrated in the diagrams below.

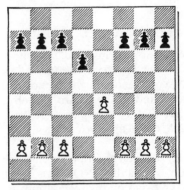

1. White's center is superior.

2. White has a strong center.

In these diagrams of "Pawn skeletons" the pieces normally on the board have been removed to make the Pawns stand out. In diagram 1, White has a Pawn at his K4 square and Black has a center Pawn at Q3. With this arrangement of Pawns, *White has secured an advantage.* In the first place, his KP is further advanced than Black's QP and attacks two important squares in enemy territory; the Pawn is an annoying and restricting force which prevents Black from placing pieces on the attacked squares. More important, the white KP is in *undisputed control of White's Q5 square.* There is no Black Pawn to prevent White from placing a piece on this square. (Black cannot dispute this control by advancing his QBP without creating a serious weakness in his Pawn position. His QP would then become an easy target for attack.) The outcome of the game in which this Pawn position exists would depend, of course, on many other factors, but White will probably be able to capitalize on his advantage by playing up his KBP and attacking on the King-side. An attack of this nature is the customary outcome of such a Pawn position.

177

Note that if Black's center Pawn in diagram 1 were at his K3 instead of Q3, White would no longer have control of his Q5 square and his advantage in the center would be greatly reduced. Furthermore, if Black's center Pawn were at his K4 square (instead of Q3) complete equality would be established.

In diagram 2, White has secured a clear and definite superiority in the center. He has all the advantages of diagram 1 plus a Pawn at Q4. Presuming that White's KP and QP cannot be captured, Black is hampered and restricted by these Pawns as he cannot place any of his pieces on central squares, or even on squares subsidiary to the center. Here, White's wedge in the center is a serious matter and may develop into an overwhelming attack.

DEVELOPING TO CONTROL THE CENTER

Every opening move should have some bearing and influence on the situation in the center. White usually starts the game by playing P–K4 or P–Q4. In either case, a center Pawn is moved, not only because two pieces (Queen and Bishop) are thereby released, but because the Pawn immediately occupies a central square. The move itself is important, quite apart from its effect on the mobility of other pieces.

If White starts with P–K4, he will, if given the opportunity to do so with advantage, follow this up by playing P–Q4 at a later stage. Against some defenses, he plays P–Q4 on his second move; against others, he tries to get this move in later. Similarly, if he starts with P–Q4 he tries to play P–K4 later. If he can place two Pawns in the center and maintain them there, he will have secured an important advantage.

Black, however, will try to equalize the condition in the center as soon as possible; he will try to prevent White from obtaining either of the Pawn arrangements in the above diagrams, or similar positions. For instance, in answer to P–K4, he may reply with the same move, playing 1 ... P–K4, which is the safest defense. This stops White from playing P–Q4 without further preparation. Black will then try to maintain his own Pawn at K4, attack and try to remove White's center Pawn, strive to play P–Q4 himself at a favorable moment, make every effort to equalize or seize control of the center.

The Pawn play in the center varies with each opening, but the point to be remembered is that *each player tries to maintain at least one of his own Pawns in the center and strives to remove his opponent's center Pawn.*

(Note that "maintaining" a Pawn in the center does not necessarily mean that the original Pawn stays in this position. A Pawn is maintained if the original Pawn is captured and a supporting Pawn takes its place. Similarly, a Pawn is "removed" only when no other Pawn can take its place by recapture.)

The importance of the center also serves as a guide to the best development of the pieces in the opening. Knights are usually played to KB3 and QB3 because in these locations they attack central squares and are ready to occupy one of these squares at a later stage, if possible.

A Bishop is often played to KKt5 or QKt5 in order to pin a Knight. The restriction of the Knight's mobility is important in itself, but the move also affects central control because the opponent's Knight is attacking the center. In some openings, a Bishop is developed at QB4 or KB4. Here it is located on one of the subsidiary center squares, directly bearing on the center and in control of a long, open diagonal. The squares on which the Bishops are developed vary with each opening. Sometimes a Bishop is placed at K3 or Q3, where it supports the center and is free to move in either direction. In other openings, one Bishop may be temporarily developed on K2 or Q2; and in still other openings, one or both Bishops may be "fianchettoed"—which means development at KKt2 or QKt2, to control the center from the wing.

It should be noted that the Bishop does not have to be placed *on* a central square to be effective. Being a long range piece, the Bishop can control from afar. All it needs is a long, open diagonal. A Knight, however, is a short-range piece and is much more powerful when placed in the center.

It should also be observed that the choice of square on which to develop a Bishop is not so easily determined as in the case of a Knight. To play Kt–B3 is a strong move in practically all positions, but it takes some time and a further revelation of the opponent's plans to decide where to develop a Bishop. For this reason, *the Knight is usually developed first.*

After the initial Pawn move, or moves, the Knight is the first piece to enter the fray. Sometimes both Knights are brought out before a Bishop is moved. On other occasions, one Knight is developed and then a Bishop, followed by the other Knight. The remaining Bishop may be developed later, but it is usually *released* so that it is free to move when the right moment arrives.

As we have pointed out, the Queen is generally held in the background until two or three minor pieces have been developed. In many openings, the Queen moves to K2 or QB2; less frequently, it is developed at Q3 or QKt3. Wherever it goes, the Queen always has an eye on the center.

After castling, the Rooks are customarily placed at K1 and Q1 where they exert pressure on the center files, a pressure which increases as exchanges take place in the center of the board. However, if there is an open file (cleared of Pawns), a Rook usually occupies it at once, particularly if the file is near the center. For instance, if the QB file is open, the QR will go to QB1 where it sweeps the file with its power. To maintain control of such an open file, the player often "doubles" his Rooks, i.e., he advances one Rook on the file and brings the other Rook behind its mate so that their power is combined on the same file.

Examples of Center Control

ON THIS and the following pages we present three illustrations of the importance of center control. The first example is an opening trap in which Black loses quickly because he gives up control of the center. In the second example, White succeeds in establishing two Pawns in the center. Black has an opportunity to break up this formation but fails to do so. As a result, White crashes through the center with a winning attack. The power of two unopposed center Pawns is clearly demonstrated. In the third illustration, White seizes an opportunity to remove his opponent's center Pawn and establishes the type of Pawn superiority given in diagram 1, page 175. The finish of the game (Pollock-Mortimer, London 1887) shows how White capitalizes on this advantage with a winning King-side attack.

In these examples, observe how each developing move is directed towards the center in an attempt to establish superiority, or at least obtain equality, in this section of the board. If an advantage in the center is secured, the game often "plays itself" thereafter.

1 This first example comes under the heading of an *opening trap*. As shown here, the starting moves are 1 P–K4, P–K4; 2 Kt–QB3, Kt–KB3; 3 P–B4. This is called the Vienna Gambit. White offers a wing Pawn to dislodge Black's center Pawn and give White a free hand in the center. *Black should not take the Pawn.*

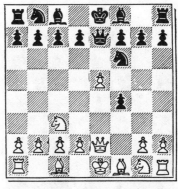

2 But here we show Black falling into the trap. He played 3 . . . PxP and White pushed on with 4 P–K5, attacking the Kt. Black hated to return his Kt to Kt1 (but this is best) and played 4 . . . Q–K2, pinning White's KP, but White then played 5 Q–K2, reaching the above position, and now Black must retreat his Kt or lose it.

3 So Black played 5 ... Kt–Kt1 and
after 6 Kt–B3, Kt–QB3; 7 P–Q4
we reach this position. Now Black
finds that he seems to have run out
of moves! He can't move either of
his Bishops; in fact, he cannot develop a single piece. What to do?
Perhaps a Pawn move to give himself some freedom? (Best move is 7
... Q–Q1.)

4 Blissfully unaware of what is going
to happen to him, Black has
played 7 ... P–Q3 with the idea of
developing his Queen–Bishop. Inci-
dentally, he hopes to get rid of that
annoying White Pawn in the center
of the board when his troubles will
be over ... but his dreams are shat-
tered as White wallops him with 8
Kt–Q5!

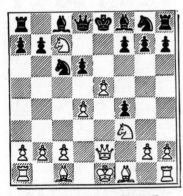

5 The Black Queen hurriedly retreated to Q1 and then White
delivered the second body punch
with 9 KtxPch! And now, after only
9 moves, Black has an irretrievably
lost game! Can one little Pawn capture bring all this trouble in its
wake? It can, when it involves giving
up control of the important central
squares.

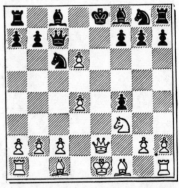

6 Black has played QxKt and White
delivered the knockout with 10
PxP, a deadly discovered check
which wins the Queen. If Black had
played 9 ... K–Q2; 10 KtxR would
also win soon. Where did Black go
wrong? In position No. 1 he should
have played 3 ... P–Q4 and if 4
PxKP, KtxP; or if 4 PxQP, either
PxP or P–K5.

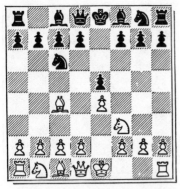

1 This example of the opening battle for control of the center has started with 1 P–K4, P–K4; 2 Kt–KB3, Kt–QB3; 3 B–B4. We have seen this opening before but the moves now take on new meaning when their purpose is understood. The Pawns occupy central squares and the force of each move is directed towards the center.

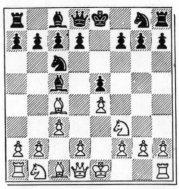

2 Black has played 3...B–B4 and the opening is now called the Giuoco Piano. (When Black plays 3...Kt–B3 it is called the Two Knights' Defense.) White has continued with 4 P–B3. This is by no means a wasted Pawn move. White intends to build up a strong center and remove Black's center Pawn with his next move.

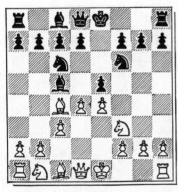

3 Black has replied with 4...Kt–B3, attacking White's K–Pawn, and White has followed up his last move with 5 P–Q4. Every move hits at the center. White is now threatening PxB as well as PxP. Note that Black's center Pawn is attacked twice, defended only once. What should Black do in this critical position?

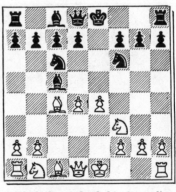

4 Black has solved his immediate problems in the only feasible way —by exchanging Pawns with 5... PxP; 6 PxP. But now White again threatens PxB. Moreover, White has succeeded in placing 2 Pawns on central squares and has removed Black's center Pawn! Black must find a way to break up White's center at once.

5 Black has played 6 ... B–Kt3 and White has attacked the Kt with 7 P–Q5. Black's Bishop move was a bad blunder, relinquishing all control of the center. He should have played 6 ... B–Kt5ch. Then if 7 Kt–B3, KtxKP removes one of White's center Pawns; or if 7 B–Q2, BxBch; 8 QKtxB, P–Q4 breaks up the center and equalizes.

6 As a result of Black's mistake, the two White Pawns will crash through the center of the line with devastating effect. Black's QKt, attacked in position 5, has retreated to K2 (the only other playable move, equally bad, was Kt–Kt1) and White has pushed on with 8 P–K5, attacking Black's other Knight. White is breaking through

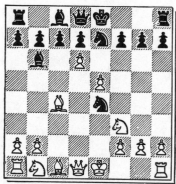

7 Hoping to get some counter-play by attacking White's KBP, Black has moved his Kt to K5—but the forward march of the center Pawns continues. White has played 9 P–Q6. The Queen Pawn now jabs at the Black Knight at K2. Note how this steamroller advance in the center sweeps aside all opposition in its path.

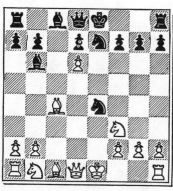

8 Black decided to get rid of one of the Pawns with the exchange 9 ... PxP; 10 PxP. There was little else he could do. In position 7, if 9 ... Kt–Kt3; 10 Q–Q5 wins the Kt at K5 as Black must guard the threat of 11 QxP mate; or if 9 ... KtxBP; 10 Q–Kt3 with a murderous attack (threat: 11 BxPch followed by 12 B–Kt5, etc.).

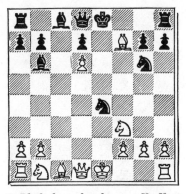

9 Black has played 10 ... Kt–Kt3.
　　White did not continue 11 Q–Q5 as Black could just castle and the open King-file prohibits 12 Qx–Kt. (11 Q–Q5, O–O; 12 QxKt? R–K1.) Instead, White has played 11 BxPch! The Pawns have done their damage and cleared the way. Now White capitalizes on his position.

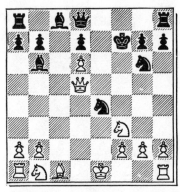

10 Black has played 11 ... KxB and White has continued 12 Q–Q5ch. Diagrams 11A and 11B show two possible continuations from this point. In position 9, if Black played 11 ... K–B1 (instead of KxB) then 12 Q–Q5, Kt–B3; 13 Q–Kt3 and White is a Pawn up with a fine position against Black's hopeless mess.

11A In position 10, if Black plays 12 ... K–B1, White captures 13 QxKt and the final position is shown above. White can now win with ease. He is a Pawn up and can get his pieces into action at once. Black is all tangled up and hemmed in. For instance, the Q–Bishop is so imprisoned that it will take four moves to get it out!

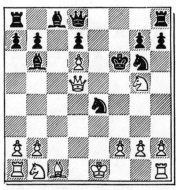

11B In position 10, if Black plays 12 ... K–B3 (to prevent QxKt by ... R–K1) he walks into a mate. As shown here, White plays 13 Kt–Kt5 and announces mate in 2. The threat is KtxKt mate. If 13 ... R–K1; 14 KtxP mate, or if 13 ... Ktx–Kt; 14 BxKt mate, and if 13 ... Kt elsewhere; 14 KtxPch RxKt: 15 B–Kt5 mate.

1 In this third example, the game has started with 1 P–K4, P–K4; 2 Kt–KB3, Kt–QB3; 3 Kt–B3. This is the first time we have seen this 3rd move for White. It usually leads to a rather drawish game. Black should answer with 3 ... Kt–B3 (Four Knights' Game) or 3 ... B–Kt5 (Three Knights' Game).

2 Black has played 3 ... B–B4 and White has captured 4 KtxP! Black's third move was a bad mistake as he immediately loses control of the center. If he had anticipated his opponent's reply he would not have made this move. White's capture looks like a sacrifice but actually it is not.

3 Black has played 4 ... KtxKt and White has followed up with 5 P–Q4! This regains the piece by a simultaneous attack on Black's Bishop and Knight. Black must give up one or the other. Note carefully this type of attack. It is a dangerous weapon and is often used to win a piece.

4 Black decided to retain his Bishop and has played 5 ... B–Q3. White has captured 6 PxKt, regaining his piece and accomplishing his object. He has not only forced Black to lose time, but has secured superiority in the center, having removed Black's center Pawn and maintained his own Pawn at K4.

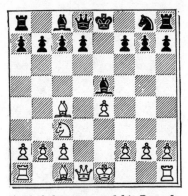

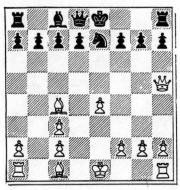

5 Black has recovered his Pawn by 6 ... BxP and White has developed his Bishop with 7 B–QB4. Note that a tempo has been gained as White has a Pawn at K4 and 2 pieces in action, whereas Black has only his Bishop to show for his opening moves. White is now in a strong position with numerous threats.

6 Fearing White's threat of P–B4 and the loss of more time with his Bishop, Black decided to exchange (7 ... BxKtch; 8 PxB) and then played 8 ... Kt–K2. White immediately seized the opportunity to attack and played 9 Q–R5, reaching this position. Now White is threatening QxP mate. Black should have played 8 ... Kt–B3.

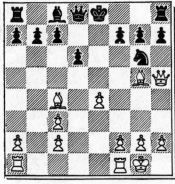

7 To defend the threat of mate, Black played 9 ... Kt–Kt3. Then White castled and Black released his QB with 10 ... P–Q3. Again White developed with a threat as he played 11 B–KKt5 attacking the Queen. Above diagram shows position after these moves. Note that White's center Pawn superiority is now the type of diagram 1, page 175.

8 Black's attacked Queen moved to Q2, causing another weakness as the Queen now blocks the Bishop, and White played 12 P–KR3 (to prevent Black from moving Q–Kt5 and exchange of Queens). Then Black castled and White has launched his K-side attack with 13 P–B4. Now the center control pays dividends.

187

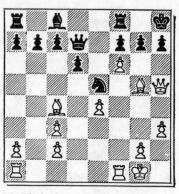

9 *Attempting to meet the oncoming assault, Black has played 13 ...K–R1 to unpin his KBP so that he can counter-attack with P–B3. But White allows no time for this and has attacked the Kt with 14 P–B5. The onward march of the Pawn sweeps away defensive pieces in its path and clears the way for the final mate.*

10 *Black has moved Kt–K4, attacking White's Bishop, but White pays no attention to this threat and pushes on with 15 P–B6! In this position, Black has no time to take the Bishop as White is threatening mate. (16 PxPch, KxP; 17 B–B6ch, K–Kt1; 18 Q–Kt5 mate. If 16 PxPch, K–Kt1; 17 PxR also leads to mate.)*

11 *Black has played P–KKt3, his only defense, and White has continued 16 Q–R6. Now he threatens Q–Kt7 or QxR mate. The white KBP has penetrated the defenses surrounding the Black King and has reached its goal. This advance of the KBP would never have been possible if Black had maintained a Pawn at K4.*

12 *Again Black has played his only defense, R–KKt1, and White has finished the game with 17 R–B4! White is now threatening QxPch, followed by R–R4 mate. There is no defense and Black resigned. All Black's troubles in this game can be traced to his 3rd move which cost a tempo and lost control of the center.*

SUMMARY OF OPENING PROCEDURE

IN THIS SECTION, we have explained the principles to be followed when selecting opening moves, but we again emphasize that *the first thing to do before making any move is to consider your opponent's threats.*

A contemplated move may do everything that a good opening move is supposed to do, but if it does not answer the opponent's threat, it is not the proper time to make the move. *Each move must be relevant to the position as it exists on the board.* If your opponent is threatening you with loss of material, your choice of moves is immediately limited to those which answer this threat. All other moves may be summarily rejected. You may be able to meet the threat with a good developing move or a good counter-attacking move, but you must answer the threat in some way, even if your reply does not meet the requirements of good development.

For instance, if you start your game with 1 P–K4 and your opponent replies with 1 ... P–Q4, your King-Pawn is attacked and something must be done about it. You may decide to exchange Pawns by playing 2 PxP (best) or you may protect your Pawn, or advance it; but you cannot ignore the threat and make an irrelevant move, no matter how good the move may be in all other respects. (An exception to this rule exists in the case of a premature attack. If you decide that the execution of your opponent's threat will gain you more than adequate compensation in development for any material loss, you may be able to ignore his threat.)

The opponent's positional threats also affect the choice of opening moves. For instance, if your opponent is trying to prevent you from castling, this threat will cause you to develop your pieces so that you will be able to castle. An ordinary developing move which does not meet this threat would be irrelevant in such a position.

Another important rule which we reiterate for emphasis is the following:

Never make a move without considering your opponent's replies.

It is essential that existing threats be answered. It is just as important to *anticipate* threats. Before making any move, visualize the reply you would make if you were playing your opponent's side of the board. Don't presume that he will make a weak answer. Give him credit for being able to find the strongest reply. In this way you will avoid making weak moves which give your opponent an opportunity to gain material or positional advantage.

Threats and counter-threats are the attacking weapons which condition the development of the pieces in the opening. The threats are not made with the expectation of winning material, but in an effort to seize control of the center and build up a strong, mobile position. Nevertheless, the threats must be answered and anticipated. If they are ignored, the resulting loss of material or positional weakness may decide the issue immediately.

A good example of how threats affect the development of pieces is found in the "Scotch Gambit" opening illustrated in the diagrams below.

 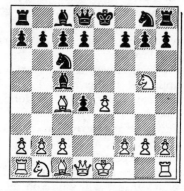

The game starts with the moves 1 P–K4, P–K4; 2 Kt–KB3, Kt–QB3; 3 P–Q4, reaching the position in the diagram at the left. This opening leads to an open type of game which Black must defend with care. However, White's 3rd move is not particularly good as he will find it difficult to maintain his King-Pawn in the center. Black is given the opportunity to capture the Queen-Pawn and should do so immediately.

The diagram at the right shows the position after the continuation 3 ... PxP; 4 B–B4, B–B4; 5 Kt–Kt5. Now White has sacrificed a Pawn for quick development and an attack against Black's KB2 square. This is a particularly vulnerable point, as the KBP is guarded only by the Black King. Many King-Pawn openings are based on an assault against this Pawn.

White is attacking the KBP with two pieces—Bishop and Knight—and is threatening to play either BxPch or KtxBP. To guard with the Queen would accomplish nothing as White would cheerfully give up Knight and Bishop for the Queen. *The best move for Black is 5 ... Kt–R3!* This guards the KBP a second time and clears the way for castling, if White permits. Note that

Kt–R3 is not a good developing move under ordinary circum-stances. A Knight is not well placed at R3. The normal develop-ment square is KB3, attacking the center. But to play Kt–B3 in this position would be completely irrelevant as White would immediately capture KtxBP and win the exchange. This threat must be met and Kt–R3 is the way to meet it, despite all theo-retical objections to the move.

Actually, White's attack is premature and gains him nothing when properly defended in this manner Thus, after 5 . . . Kt–R3; 6 KtxBP, KtxKt; 7 BxKtch, KxB; 8 Q–R5ch, P–Kt3; 9 QxB, P–Q4, Black has slightly the better of it. However, many a game has been won by this type of attack against inferior defense.

DEVELOP WITH THREATS

The principles of good opening procedure can be summarized in one sentence:

Bring out all your pieces as quickly as possible, placing them on strong squares, and play to get control of the center.

What does it mean to develop a piece on a strong square? The answer to this question has already been given. In its new loca-tion, the piece must be *free from harmful attack*; on the next move, or shortly thereafter, the opponent must not be able to drive the piece away with a strong reply and gain a tempo. Furthermore, the Principle of Mobility must be observed; the piece should not interfere with the development of your other men. If these conditions are met, a piece which attacks the center directly, or helps to control the center, is developed on a strong square.

It is possible, however, that two or more moves may conform to the requirements outlined above. In such cases, each move is probably playable and the selection is a matter of choice. But there is an additional rule which may aid your selection: the best move is *the one which hurts your opponent the most*. Select a move which gives your opponent a problem to solve. Attack one of his pieces, or a vulnerable square; pin one of his Knights or otherwise restrict his mobility; threaten to win material or create a weakness in his position.

By making a sound developing move which attacks or threatens something, you limit your opponent's choice of replies. You may force him to make a defensive move which does not aid his de-velopment. His answer may even interfere with his mobilization and cramp his position. You also give him an opportunity to make a mistake. If he does not answer your threat in the best way, you may gain an immediate advantage.

The "threat" factor is often most important in deciding *the right time* to develop a piece. Every effort should be made to time your opening moves so that the full force of each piece is released when it is developed. Every move cannot embody a threat, but if a choice exists, select the move which meets all the conditions of sound development and at the same time does the most damage to your opponent's position.

OPENING VARIATIONS

Someone once went to the trouble of trying to calculate the number of possible moves in a game of chess. He discovered that the number of possible ways of playing *the first ten moves* amounted to the astronomical figure of 169,518,829,100,544,000,-000,000,000,000!

Does this mean that the chess openings are so complex that the average person can never hope to be able to play the game? Emphatically not! It merely means that chess is a game of infinite possibilities and permits each player to give free rein to his imagination in the choice of moves and determination of playing strategy. It means, too, that chess is a game of delightful variety. No two games are alike!

However, it also means that it is practically impossible to *memorize* all the chess openings, especially if one includes all the inferior possibilities for each player. Chess simply cannot be played by rote. Players who laboriously memorize opening variations recommended by chessmasters usually find themselves completely at sea if the opponent deviates from "the book." The important thing is to understand the objectives of the opening and to adhere to the principles outlined in this chapter. Let these principles be your guide in selecting a move in each position.

Actually, in any given position, the choice of moves is definitely limited. Most of the possible moves are obviously bad, even to a beginner at the game. When these bad moves are weeded out, the choice usually boils down to *just a few moves*. The real question is how to choose one of the three or four playable moves which are actually available. The principles we have outlined will aid you in making this choice. When it is your turn to move, think in the following terms:

1. *What does he threaten?* Always ask this first. If there is a threat, your next move must answer it.

2. *Can I remove my opponent's center Pawn?* If you have been given this opportunity, remove the Pawn, provided you will not lose material or be exposed to mate.

3. *What developing moves are available to me which aid in the control of the center?* You will find that only a few moves answer these requirements. Consider them and give preference to the one which does the most harm to your opponent's position.

4. *What is his best reply?* Check the merits of each contemplated move by considering your opponent's best replies. Select and make the move to which he has no really strong reply.

Follow the above procedure and you are much more likely to pick a good move and get good opening development than by trying to remember the "book" move in any position.

Players who wish to take part in competitive chess events will undoubtedly find it advisable and helpful to make a study of opening variations. For these players and other students of the game, some excellent books, devoted solely to the interesting subject of the chess openings, are available. However, any attempt by the beginner to "analyze" the openings usually produces a state of mental fog. For this reason, we do not include in the present work any list of opening variations. Such a list would be beyond the scope of this introduction to chess.

When you have gained sufficient experience in actual play you may find it beneficial to study the objectives and lines of play in specific openings. Meantime, the illustrative games throughout this book will provide you with enough examples to give you a working knowledge of opening procedure.

HOW DEVELOPMENT WINS

THERE IS no such thing as a "forced win" at the start of a game of chess. If there were, all interest would be removed from the game. White has the first move and therefore possesses the initiative, but this is not sufficient to force a win. Black cannot afford to be too aggressive in the opening and must play with care to prevent White from increasing the slight advantage conferred by the opening move, but if both sides develop their pieces properly, there is no logical reason for one to beat the other.

Many well-played games between strong players end in a draw; others are won because one player is able to accumulate minute advantages in his position which finally result in gaining material. Between ordinary players, however, most games are won as a result of blunders (called "oversights" when made by masters) or *because the loser failed to develop his pieces in the opening.*

The rules for opening development are comparatively simple —but how few players observe these rules! Masters continue to give odds of a Knight or a Rook to amateurs, and trounce them decisively, mainly because the master brings all his pieces out quickly and posts them on strong squares where they do the most damage. He takes into account, too, his opponent's possibilities of development. If the amateur threatens to place a piece on a good square, the master advances a Pawn and prevents it—or he drives away pieces which have reached good squares if they are not properly supported.

How does the amateur conduct his game? He brings out two or three pieces and then begins to look around for combinations! He never finds them, because they cannot possibly be there! When he loses, he attributes it to the master's superhuman powers of calculation and shows you how the combination which won the game was foreseen thirty moves back. Actually, nothing of the sort takes place. Masters do make wonderful combinations, but they are usually based on superior development. When all the pieces are developed, and the opponent's are not, combinations do not have to be sought. They are there on the premises, ready and waiting.

One-time world champion Wilhelm Steinitz was once asked: "How can you give odds of a Rook and still win so easily?" Steinitz answered: "Look at my opponent's position. His Queen-Rook, Knight and Bishop are still home on their original squares. He's really giving me Rook odds, and nobody in the world can do that!"

To illustrate how development wins, we present two beautiful games played by masters. The first is a famous encounter by Paul Morphy against the Duke of Brunswick and Count Isouard. The combinations are really exquisite and the Queen sacrifice which forces checkmate is delightful. It is almost a shame to take you behind the scenes and show you that the "brilliant" moves are simply the application of cold logic in the treatment of the opponent's violation of proper principles of development. In this game you will see the following important ideas carried out by Morphy, playing White:

1. Rapid development of all the pieces.

2. Sacrifice as a means of tearing open the adversary's position.

3. How to conduct an attack against a badly developed position.

4. How to intensify pressure against pieces that are pinned.

5. The power of Rooks on open files.

6. The importance of getting one's King into safety quickly by castling early in the game.

The second illustration is an almost perfect example of precise and logical development by the player of the white pieces, grandmaster Akiba Rubinstein, who won the game in 1920 at Gothenberg against chessmaster Maroczy. Superior development enables White to break through brilliantly but logically on the King-side and force checkmate.

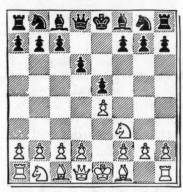

1 The game has started with 1 P–K4, P–K4; 2 Kt–KB3, P–Q3. Note that White's 2nd move is the only sound developing move which attacks the center and also threatens something. Black's response is inferior as he neglected the opportunity to answer the threat by developing a piece. (...Kt–QB3 or ...Kt–KB3.)

2 White continued 3 P–Q4, attacking Black's K–Pawn twice, and Black has defended with B–Kt5, pinning the Kt. Again Black's reply is bad. His Bishop is not posted on a strong square because he cannot maintain the pin after White's next move. It is too early to develop the Bishop. Relatively better is Kt–QB3, Kt–Q2 or PxP.

3 White has captured 4 PxP and Black has replied with BxKt, the only way to avoid losing a Pawn. (If 4...PxP; 5 QxQch, KxQ; 6 KtxP.) This demonstrates that Black's original Bishop move was not a good developing move and not the right way to answer White's threat. The Bishop moved twice and lost a tempo.

4 White has played 5 QxB and Black has recaptured his Pawn. In this position it is White's turn to move and Black has nothing to show in the way of development for his opening moves. Two bad moves have cost him time and given White a superior position. White's Queen is strongly posted and not subject to attack.

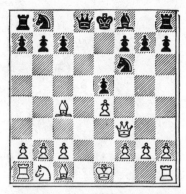

5 White continued 6 B–QB4 and Black replied with Kt–KB3. Note that White developed his Bishop with a threat (QxP mate) and that the Bishop is now posted on a strong square, subsidiary to the center, attacking Black's vulnerable KB2 square. Black defended the threat of mate by developing a piece.

6 Now White has played 7 Q–QKt3, threatening BxPch and mate with the Queen, which Black has defended with Q–K2. Black did not play Q–Q2 as then White could continue with QxP and win Black's Rook. White is not attacking prematurely. His opponent's inferior opening play gave White time to move his Queen twice.

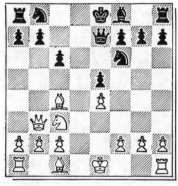

7 White has developed another piece and guarded his KP with 8 Kt–B3 and Black has defended White's threat of QxP (winning the Rook) by playing P–B3. In position 6, White could have won a Pawn by playing 8 QxP but Black would have responded with Q–Kt5ch, forcing exchange of Queens and killing the attack.

8 White has released the full force of his other Bishop by playing 9 B–KKt5, pinning the opponent's Kt, and Black, in desperation, has countered with P–Kt4, but this is a bad move. Note that White is fully developed, ready to castle, while Black is in a hopeless tangle with only one piece in play and that one is pinned.

9 White has played 10 KtxP! With such an imposing lead in development and mobility, White can afford to make this sacrifice of a piece to maintain his aggressive position. To have backed away with his Bishop would have permitted Black to extricate himself by moving his Queen, developing his Bishop and castling.

10 Black has accepted the sacrifice, capturing PxKt, and White has recaptured with 11 BxKtPch. Now White has taken 2 Pawns in exchange for his Knight and has held on to his mobile, threatening position, giving his opponent no opportunity to untangle his pieces and move his King out of danger.

11 Black got out of check by playing QKt–Q2 and White has followed up with 12 O–O–O, thereby safeguarding his King and at the same time bringing the QR into active play on the open file where it attacks Black's pinned Knight! Another example of developing with an attack as White now threatens BxKtch!

12 In position 11, White's threat of BxKtch was undefended as Black's King could not recapture, the Queen dare not, and the other Knight is paralyzed by White's Bishop! So Black has played R–Q1; but White gives him no rest and has sacrificed the exchange with 13 RxKt! Again Black's response is forced.

13 Black recaptured RxR and White has played 14 R–Q1. Now we see that the sacrifice of the exchange has brought the other Rook into action without loss of time and cut down one of the pieces defending the Black King. White now threatens to capture the pinned Rook. In chess you can hit a man when he's down.

14 Black has played Q–K3 to unpin his Knight and enable this piece to recapture without losing his Queen. White has continued with 15 BxRch. This is the first move in a combination to force checkmate. White is chopping down the defenders and hacking his way through to final victory in spectacular fashion.

15 Black recaptured KtxB, his only means of avoiding material loss, and White has played 16 Q–Kt8ch!! Still another sacrifice, and one which Black must accept as he has no other way of getting out of check. In a well planned combination the opponent's moves must be forced and the outcome clearly foreseen.

16 Black has captured KtxQ, his only move, and White has mated with 17 R–Q8. This game demonstrates convincingly and delightfully the triumph of development and mobility over mere dead weight. Black has lost even though he is far ahead in material with most of his remaining pieces set up for the next game!

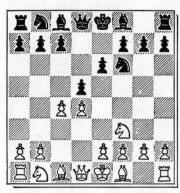

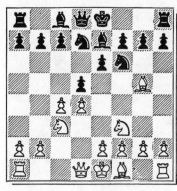

1 This second example of how superior development wins started with 1 P–Q4, Kt–KB3; 2 Kt–KB3, P–Q4; 3 P–B4, P–K3; known as the Orthodox Defense of the Queen's Gambit Declined. White offered his QBP to gain center control but here Black declined and guarded his QP. If accepted, White could easily regain the Pawn.

2 The game has continued with 4 B–Kt5, B–K2; 5 Kt–B3, QKt–Q2, reaching this position. Note how White develops a different piece with each move and how each move increases the pressure on Black's center Pawn. Moreover, every move attacks or restricts and the pieces are all posted on strong squares.

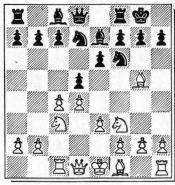

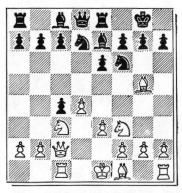

3 To release his KB and reinforce his QP, White continued 6 P–K3; then Black castled and White has played 7 R–B1. This Rook occupies an important file and prevents Black from playing ...P–B4 to obtain freedom. (If 7...P–B4; 8 Px-BP, PxP; 9 P–B6, Kt–Kt3; 10 Kt–K5 with a strong positional advantage.)

4 In position 3, Black's best move is P–B3 to keep the QB-file closed—but in this game Black played R–K1. Then White developed his Queen with 8 Q–B2 and Black played PxP. Black is too impatient. His position is cramped but quite playable. The Pawn exchange only helps White. Again, 8...P–B3 was best.

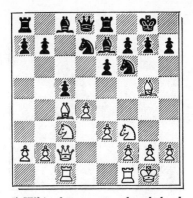

5 White has recaptured and developed a piece at the same time by playing 9 BxP. Then Black moved P–B4 and White castled (10 O–O). Black is attempting to free his game but it is extremely dangerous for him to open up the QB-file and the Q-file as White can command both files and attack.

6 Black captured PxP and White recaptured with 11 KtxP. Then Black played P–QR3 and White finished his development with 12 KR–Q1. Now look at White's position. Every piece is developed on a strong square before any attempt at attack is made and each piece was developed with one move.

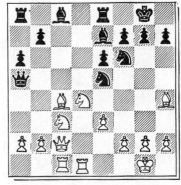

7 Not yet fully developed, Black's last few moves were weak and exposed him to dangerous attacks on the two open files. Realizing his Queen was vulnerable, he played Q–R4, attacking White's Bishop across the board. White moved 13 B–R4 and Black attacked the other Bishop with Kt–K4. This was a good move but the follow-up is bad.

8 White preserved his Bishop and unblocked the QB-file by playing 14 B–K2 and Black responded with Kt–Kt3, attacking the other Bishop. White then moved 15 B–Kt3, commanding a long diagonal but Black closed the line and attacked White's Knight with P–K4. (Black should have played 14 ... Kt–B3. His Kt is needed on the Q-side.)

9 White moved 16 Kt–Kt3, attacking Black's Queen. Desperately searching for a place of safety, the Queen retreated to B2. But White continued 17 Q–Kt1 and now the Black Queen faces the Rook's fire, veiled by the Kt, and must flee. White threatens Kt–Kt5, followed by Kt–B7 winning the exchange.

10 Black's Queen retreated to Kt1 and White has played 18 B–B3, transferring this Bishop to an attacking post where it pins Black's QKtP. Note that although both Queens are at Kt1 squares, Black's strongest piece interferes with his QR while White's Rooks are not hampered by the Queen.

11 To release his QR, Black played Q–R2. White then attacked the QKtP a second time with 19 Kt–R5 so that Black's QB cannot move and leave the Pawn unprotected. To chase away the annoying Kt, Black has countered with B–QKt5. But White's maneuver was made to transfer the Kt to a better square.

12 White moved 20 Kt–B4 and at last Black was able to develop his Bishop by playing B–Q2. Pressing home his positional advantage with attacking moves, White has played 21 Kt–Q5. Now he threatens Kt–B7, winning the exchange, or KtxKtch followed by RxB, or simply KtxB. Obviously, Black must remove the Kt.

13 Black captured KtxKt and White recaptured 22 BxKt. Then Black played B–K3 to meet White's threat of BxPch followed by RxB. White did not exchange, as that would help Black, but brought another piece out with 23 Q–K4. Note that it is often better to let the opponent capture and occupy a strong square on recapturing.

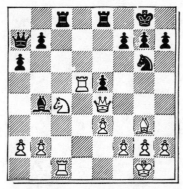

14 To reduce White's forces and eliminate the attack on his QKtP, Black captured BxB and White recaptured by 24 RxB. Now Black has finally brought his QR into the game by playing QR–B1. Black is now pinning White's Knight to prevent him from playing KtxP. But White prepared for this on his last move.

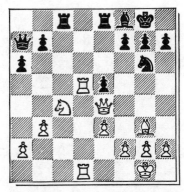

15 White released the pin and doubled Rooks on the Q-file with 25 QR–Q1. He also threatened KtxP with a disclosed attack by the Queen on the Black Bishop. Black replied by playing B–B1. Now White has guarded his Kt by 26 P–Kt3 to release his Queen. (Black was threatening P–B4, followed by P–B5.)

16 In an attempt to get his Queen into the game, Black played P–Kt4, attacking the Kt. White countered with 27 Kt–Q6. Now the Knight is attacking both Rooks and threatening to win the exchange. Note that White could not play 27 KtxP as this would lose a piece. Thus, if 27 KtxP, P–B3 and the pinned Kt is lost.

17 The response to White's last move was forced and Black played BxKt. White recaptured by 28 RxB. Now Black has played R–B2. His object is to prevent White from continuing R–Q7, attacking the Queen and occupying the 7th rank. This is the strongest location for a Rook in the mid-game.

18 White has begun the final attack which wins the game. He played 29 P–KR4, threatening P–R5 followed by BxP. Black replied by defending his KP with P–B3. (If . . . P–KR4 White would win the RP with Q–B5.) White has continued 30 Q–Q5ch and now completely dominates the board.

19 Black got out of check by playing K–R1 and White has attacked the Knight with 31 P–R5. In a mating attack every move must be forceful and give the opponent no opportunity to assemble his pieces in defense of his King. By attacking the Knight, White gains time for his next move—to which there is no good answer.

20 Black moved his Kt to B1 and White has played 32 P–R6! His object is to break up the Pawn barricade surrounding the Black King. In other games we have seen the same technique. Now if Black plays PxP White would soon mate: e.g. 32 . . . PxP; 33 RxBP, R–Q2; 34 BxP! RxQ; 35 RxKt dbl ch and mate!

21 Black realized he could not capture and returned his Kt to Kt3. White has continued 33 Q–K6! A brilliant Queen sacrifice? By no means. Impossible-looking moves can always be looked for when a player's position is vastly superior. Of course, if Black captures RxQ White can force mate with R–Q8ch.

22 White's only reason for his spectacular Queen move was to bring this piece into the game with decisive result. Black has moved his Rook to KB1 and White has played 34 R–Q7! Now the Rook occupies the 7th rank and White is threatening PxP mate! How can Black defend this threat? By exchanging Rooks?

23 If Black exchanged Rooks the threat of PxP mate would still be there and the Black Queen would be attacked as well. Therefore Black was forced to play PxP and now White has continued with the beautiful move B–R4!! (Threat: 36 Bx-Pch, RxB; 37 QxRch, K–Kt1; 38 Q–Kt7 mate.) This sacrifice decides the issue.

24 Again Black had no option. He was forced to capture the Bishop with his Knight. White has played his final move 36 Q–K7 and Black resigned. White threatens three mates with QxRP, Q–Kt7 or QxR and Black is defenseless. This entire game is a beautiful example of masterful play by White.

Chess Combinations

The

ARTISTRY

of CHESS

WHEN THE PIECES have been developed, the opening stage of a chess game is completed and the "middle-game" begins. The mobilized forces join in mortal combat. The officers and men of the opposing armies attack and counter-attack. The chess General fights for room to maneuver, tries to restrict his opponent's mobility, seeks to inflict losses on the enemy, brings pressure to bear on weak points in the line, pins down enemy units and concentrates his fire on them, tries to break through the defensive crust of Pawns, holds his own line intact to prevent a breakthrough, counters an assault on one flank by attacking in the center, or on the opposite wing.

In the middle-game, nearly all the tactics of warfare are reproduced on the chessboard. This is the period in which the issue may be decided by a successful assault on the enemy King. It is the phase of the game in which the brilliant, sacrificial combinations take place—the beautiful conceptions which have been called "the poetry of the chessboard."

But if the opposing armies inflict serious casualties on each other and the Kings survive the battles of the middle-game, the final "end-game" begins. With the armies reduced to skeletons of their original strength, the outcome may then be decided by the respective disposition of approximately even forces, or by a slight advantage in material.

To explain in detail the strategy, tactics and technique of the middle-game and end-game would require much more space than is available in this invitation to chess. This book has accomplished its purpose if it has clarified the rules and basic principles of the Royal Game. In these concluding pages, however, we present some examples of chess tactics and combinations, in the hope that these glimpses of the beauty and artistry of chess may add to your enjoyment of this noble game and inspire you to learn more about it.

A CHESS COMBINATION

A COMBINATION is a series of moves, usually including a sacrifice, which results in an advantage for the player who makes the combination. The opponent's replies must be more or less forced. The diagrams below show how a combination evolves.

1 White's Bishop at QKt2 is aiming in the direction of the Black King. White visualizes the possibility of producing the arrangement of diagram 2.

2 If he could clear the diagonal until only his Knight intervenes between the King and his Bishop, White could play Kt–B6 dis.ch. and win the Queen.

3 Position after 1 P–QB5, PxBP; 2 QPxP, BxPch. Having found a method of producing the position he desires, White has completed the first step of his combination. He has cleared his own Pawn from the diagonal. Black's responses were logical and gained him a Pawn.

4 Position after 3 RxB!, RxR; 4 P–Kt5, Kt–Q2. By attacking the Knight, White has cleared the diagonal and reached the position he visualized. Now he can play 5 Kt–B6 dis.ch. and win Black's Queen. If Black had made another move instead of 4 ... Kt–Q2, then 5 PxKtch. wins material.

209

THE ADVANTAGE gained by a combination may be the winning of a Pawn or piece, or even checkmate of the King. The usefulness of playing a combination, when you can, is that you are enabled to foresee your adversary's possible replies, and can plan your game accordingly.

1 It is Black's turn to move. He must act quickly as he is two exchanges behind and his King is threatened with disaster if White is allowed to play Q–K8ch. Black's Bishop is also attacked by a Pawn.

2 Black had no time to move his Bishop away, but his pieces are all aimed at the White King and a combination is in the air. Foreseeing that the outcome will be favorable, Black has played BxPch.

3 White was forced to play KxB and Black has continued with Q–Kt5ch. Now if White moves K–R1, Black will mate by Q–B6. The Bishop sacrifice has brought White's King out into the open.

4 White moved his King to B1 and Black followed up with Q–B6ch. Now White's only move is K–K1 and Black will then play Q–B7 mate. Black foresaw all this when he made the first move of this mating combination.

A COMBINATION in chess is similar to a knock-out in a fight. A fighter may lose every round on points, but if he can deliver one knock-out punch the battle is over and the point-score is unimportant. In chess, a player may be behind in material, or may sacrifice material, but he wins the game if he can achieve his object—a knock-out by checkmate.

1 *It is White's turn to move. Things don't look too bright as he is a piece behind and his opponent threatens to simplify by exchanging Queens. White's Bishop is also attacked by the Black Knight. Only a combination can save White's game.*

2 To start his combination, White has sacrificed his Queen! This position was reached after 1 QxPch, KtxQ. The sacrifice has broken the cordon of Pawns around the Black King and now White's Rook and Bishop attack the Knight.

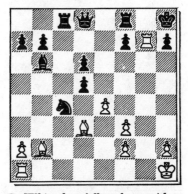

3 White has followed up with 2 RxKtch and Black was forced to move his King to R1. How should White continue his attack? An ordinary discovered check (say 3 RxBPch) would not do as Black could play KtxB.

4 But White has played 3 R–Kt8 with a double check by Rook and Bishop and Black must capture the Rook with his King to get out of check. After 3 ...KxR; 4 R–Kt1ch, Q–Kt4; 5 RxQ is mate.

IF THERE were no such thing as a combination in chess, White would win in the position of diagram 1 below. His plus of three Pawns, and his powerful Rook, easily outweigh his opponent's Knight and Bishop. To begin with, Black would have to give up a piece to stop White's passed Pawn from queening; the material thus gained would assure White an easy win. But "position" counts as much as material.

1 It is Black's move and he must evolve a combination. Defensive play will lose slowly but surely. However, Black's pieces are well placed for attack and he can force a win.

2 As shown above, Black has begun his combination by playing B–Kt7ch. An important point to remember is that a check can often force a move you want your opponent to make.

3 Calculating the possible replies is easy when, as in this case, the opponent has only one answer. White had to capture the Bishop with his Rook—and now Black has played Q–B8ch.

4 Again White had only one legal reply and returned his Rook to Kt1. Black followed up with Kt–Kt6ch. Now White's Rook is pinned and he must play PxKt. Whereupon, the pretty combination ends with Q–R6 mate.

When we speak of a player's "position" as being better, we mean that his pieces have great mobility, and are centrally posted, so that the chances are good for winning the game by direct combination. One of the principles of chess strategy is that a superiority in position must be established before venturing on a combination, or it will react unfavorably.

1 Black is to play, and there is no doubt of the superiority of his position. His Rooks are doubled, controlling the only open file, and his Knight is posted powerfully at Q5, interfering with White's pieces.

2 Black sees an opportunity to win by a mating combination. As the first step, he has played 1 ... Kt–K7ch and White has moved his King out of check, playing 2 K–R1. This was the object of Black's first move.

3 As the second step, Black has played 2 ... QxKt! He is sacrificing his Queen to remove the obstructing Knight and clear the road for his other pieces. White must accept the sacrifice or lose a piece without compensation.

4 White played 3 PxQ and Black has followed up with R–R4ch, the third step in his combination. Now Black is sacrificing his Rook, but material doesn't count if checkmate can be forced. White must play 4 PxR and then Black will conclude with R–R5 mate.

213

ONE OF THE beauties of combination play is that an apparently lost game may be saved and defeat turned into victory by an accurately planned series of forcing moves. The enemy is given no time to pursue his own designs. He may need only one move to accomplish his object, but if he is kept on the run he will never be able to make that move.

1 It is White's turn to move and the game should end in a draw. Material is equal, but Black has a slight advantage in position, as his Queen and Rook are well placed. However, White thinks he can checkmate Black.

2 White played 1 R–K7, threatening QxP mate, but this gave Black the opportunity to play a winning combination, and he has moved Q–R8ch, sacrificing his Queen! White must accept the sacrifice.

3 White had to play 2 KxQ and Black has followed up with B–B6ch. As he is himself menaced with mate, Black must force White's replies with every move of this combination. He cannot afford waiting moves.

4 Forced to make his only legal move, White played 3 K–Kt1 and Black has moved R–Q8ch. Now White is defenseless as after 4 R–K1, RxR is mate. White's original Rook move made this possible.

THE AVERAGE player may see as many good moves as the master, but there is a difference in their conduct of a game. When the ordinary player sees a promising plan, but one seemingly impossible to fulfill, he hesitates, then changes his plan. The master, on the other hand, tries to make the project possible and does so by making surprise moves, which are in reality only logical moves.

1 White is to play and he must act fast, as he is the exchange down. If he could play Kt–K7ch, driving the King to the corner, he could then get at him, but Black's Queen guards the K7 square, so how can the Knight get there?

2 White has played 1 B–Kt5! He sacrifices his Bishop to force the Black Queen away from control of the important K7 square. Black must accept the sacrifice as 1 . . . Q–B1 exposes Black to a Knight fork (2 Kt–K7ch, winning the Q).

3 Black was forced to capture the Bishop and this position was reached after 1 . . . QxB; 2 Kt–K7ch, K–R1. The Black King has been driven into the corner, but how should White continue? 3 R–R1 is too slow, as it gives Black time for defense.

4 Instead, White has played 3 QxPch! Another sacrifice which Black must accept. To get out of check, Black must now play KxQ and then 4 R–R1 is checkmate! The King's only escape squares are covered by White's Knight at K7.

215

WHEN YOU embark on a combination, it is important to watch the order in which you make your moves. A seemingly unimportant transposition may create a loophole through which the enemy King is sure to slip while you are trying to weave a mating net.

1 White is to move. He has one piece less, but has a strong attack. However, he must proceed with care. 1 KtPxP, threatening P–B8, would be answered by R–B1. Or if White plays 1 QxPch, the Black King would slip out via Q3.

2 With perfect timing, White has played 1 P–QB5! This plugs up the leaks in the position. Now White is threatening 2 QxP mate as the Black King cannot escape. Moreover, Black's Queen is attacked, giving him no time to defend with R–B1.

3 To save his Queen and defend the threatened mate, Black captured QxP, his only playable move. White has continued with 2 QxPch and this will force Black to play K–Q3. Then White will complete his combination.

4 After 2 ... K–Q3, White played 3 Kt–K4ch and now we see the object of the combination. Black's King and Queen have been forced to occupy squares on which they are now forked by White's Kt, winning Black's Queen. Here 3 ... PxKt is illegal as the Pawn is pinned.

WHEN YOUR pieces are in the vicinity of the other player's King, look for a combination. It may be necessary to give up a great deal of material to effect a breakthrough, but the object of the game is checkmate and no sacrifice is too great if that object can be attained.

1 White has all his pieces in the field, but how does he get at the King? Seemingly his pieces are in each other's way, but if he can get rid of his Knight quickly, his Rook and Bishops will have great scope.

2 Quick action calls for a check with the Knight. White has played 1 Kt–K7ch, clearing a path for his Rook, whether the Knight be taken or not. But Black must accept the sacrifice as if 1 ... K–R1; 2 QxR mate.

3 Black played QxKt and White continued 2 QxRPch! This sacrifice gives Black no chance to defend himself. To have played 2 R–R5 instead would have been faulty timing as Black could defend with 2 ... P–B4 (not 2 ... PxR; 3 QxRP mate).

4 Black was forced to play KxQ and White continued his combination with 3 R–R5ch. The Rook is immune as Black's KtP is pinned. Now Black must play 3 ... K–Kt1 and then 4 R–R8 is mate. Sound sacrifices and perfect timing featured this beautiful combination.

A DELIGHTFUL mating combination which occurs quite often is called the "smothered mate." All it needs is a Queen and Knight, and of course the opponent's King. By sacrificing the Queen, the King is forced into a position where he is smothered by his own pieces and can be checkmated by the Knight.

1 White is to move. He has sacrificed several pieces in order to reach this situation, as he has foreseen the possibility of forcing the win by a "smothered mate."

2 As in most combinations, a check serves to limit the choice of reply and force the desired position. White played 1 Kt–B7ch and Black moved K–K1, his only legal reply.

3 White could have captured the Rook but he is after bigger game. He played 2 Kt–Q6 dis.ch. and Black was forced to respond with K–Q1 as 2 ... K–B1 would have permitted 3 Q–B7 mate.

4 Then White played the startling 3 Q–K8ch! This sacrifice forces Black to play RxQ (as KxQ is illegal) and Black's King is then smothered by his own pieces. The final move is 4 Kt–B7 mate.

COMBINATIONS are not confined to any one phase of the game. They occur in the opening, mid-game or ending. If your pieces are on good squares and your opponent has a cramped or badly developed game, look for a combination as a means of realizing on your superior position.

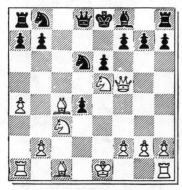

1 White to play. He is a piece ahead, but his Queen and Knight are both attacked by Black Pawns. It looks as though he must lose back a piece, but there must be a combination as the White men dominate the board.

2 White has played 1 B–Kt5ch. Now if 1...KtxB; 2 QxBP is mate. Or if 1...Kt–B3; 2 Q–B3, PxKt; 3 KtxKt, PxKt; 4 BxPch etc. Or if 1...Kt–Q2; 2 BxKtch, QxB; 3 Q–B4, Q moves; 4 QxP and White wins.

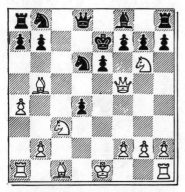

3 As all his alternatives were bad, Black has played K–K2, still trying to win back a piece with one of his Pawns. But White has countered with 2 Kt–Kt6ch! To get out of check, Black must capture the Kt, but if 2...BPxKt; 3 B–Kt5 is mate.

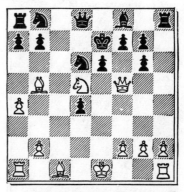

4 So Black was forced to take the Knight with his RP. With his Queen still standing en prise, White has brought up his other Kt and has played 3 Kt–Q5ch! Now Black must play 3...PxKt and then White will conclude the combination with 4 Q–K5 mate.

CHESS DOES NOT always require an opponent. You can enjoy by yourself the masterpieces produced by the world's greatest experts by playing over their games from the scores published in chess books and magazines. Another form of chess solitaire is to solve composed problems and endings. These are intended for both entertainment and instruction. A composed ending is presented below.

1 In this ending the terms are "White to Play and Win." Even to draw looks hopeless as Black's passed Pawn has only two squares to travel and there seems to be no way to stop its march.

2 White has played 1 Kt–B6 which for the moment stops the Pawn, as 1 ... P–R7 would be answered by 2 Kt–Kt4ch, followed by capturing the Pawn. But White's Knight can be captured.

3 Black removed the Knight with his King and White has played 2 B–B6. Now White threatens BxP, when his Bishop would control the diagonal and prevent Black's RP from queening. Black must meet this threat.

4 Black played K–Q4, to protect his QP, and White has played 3 P–Q3. Note that Black could not afford to play K–B4 (instead of K–Q4) as then White would have checked with his Bishop at K7 and won the RP.

5 Black has advanced his RP, playing 3 ... P–R7 and threatening to queen with check on his next move. White has countered by playing 4 P–B4ch. Now Black dare not play PxP en passant as White would just recapture BxP with a winning game.

6 Black got out of check by playing K–B4, his only means of keeping the QP guarded and preventing White from playing BxP. But now Black is threatening to queen his RP on the next move! How can White possibly win this game?

7 To avoid the threatened check, and for other good reasons, White played 5 K–Kt7 and Black queened his Pawn. Actually, White has forced Black to advance his Pawn, as any King move would have permitted 6 BxP.

8 For a moment it looked bad for White. He has only a Bishop against a Queen. But in position 7 it was White's turn to move, which makes all the difference. He played 6 B–K7, as shown above, and it's mate!

ABOUT THE AUTHORS

IRVING CHERNEV is a chess master who has taken part in state and United States Championship tournaments. Among his other books are the remarkable *Logical Chess, Move by Move* (perhaps the most instructive chess book ever written), *1000 Best Short Games of Chess* and many others. Mr. Chernev has replayed nearly every game of chess on record and is known as the "Believe It or Not" man of chess.

KENNETH HARKNESS learned to play chess as a boy in Scotland. After an early career in the world of radio, he has devoted the past twenty years to the intensive promotion and development of chess playing in the United States. He is the inventor of a numerical system of ranking chess players which has been officially adopted by the United States and British Chess Federations. Mr. Harkness is the author of the *Official Blue Book and Encyclopedia of Chess* and *Invitation to Bridge.*